As Good As It Gets

www.penguin.co.uk

Also by Romesh Ranganathan

STRAIGHT OUTTA CRAWLEY

As Good As It Gets

Life Lessons from a Reluctant Adult

ROMESH RANGANATHAN

BANTAM PRESS

TRANSWORLD PUBLISHERS
Penguin Random House, One Embassy Gardens,
8 Viaduct Gardens, London SW11 7BW
www.penguin.co.uk

Transworld is part of the Penguin Random House group of companies
whose addresses can be found at global.penguinrandomhouse.com

Penguin
Random House
UK

First published in Great Britain in 2020 by Bantam Press
an imprint of Transworld Publishers

A CIP catalogue record for this book
is available from the British Library.

ISBNS
9781787633599 (hb)
9781787633605 (tpb)

Typeset in 13.5/16 pt Garamond MT Std by Jouve (UK), Milton Keynes
Printed and bound in Great Britain by Clays Ltd, Elcograf S.p.A.

Penguin Random House is committed to a sustainable
future for our business, our readers and our planet. This book
is made from Forest Stewardship Council® certified paper.

This book is dedicated to my wife Leesa and our wonderful children, although you still haven't read the last one so I don't know why I bother. Also, it was me who broke the washing machine.

Contents

Outmanoeuvred

I want to be absolutely crystal clear on this – I am not in any position to be offering anybody advice. But that is exactly why I think I am well placed to do so. I have spent many years reading books advising you how to be more productive, how to be happy, how to crush your goals, and the one thing that has struck me about all of them is that these people are proffering advice from a position of having it nailed. I definitely do not have it nailed. In fact, I think it's fair to say that I am finding new ways to remove the nails and drive them into my own face.

This isn't a book of philosophical pontifications on life. It's more a series of musings on what I think about where I am right now, which is the thought process of a lot of men my age, just before they decide they're going to change their hairstyle, buy a motorbike or leave their wife. I like my hair, I'd kill myself on a bike, and there is no way any other woman would have me. When I started this book, I hoped it would be something people could relate to and would make them feel better about things. Then I got to the middle of it and I just hoped it would be amusing. As I approached the final third, all I wanted was to finish the fucking thing. The truth is, like all of us, I properly struggle with adulthood, and am making judgement errors every single day.

On our last holiday to Portugal, we started to get frustrated by the fact that our kids were not eating things they themselves had ordered. I wouldn't mind if those things turned up and were horrible, or even significantly different to how they were advertised. What I do find maddening is when you watch your child order something, that thing arrives, exactly as it looks on the menu, and then your child informs you that they won't be eating anything because the nuggets 'smell different'.

My first instinct is to say, 'Hold your nose then, dickhead', because it feels like our kids are being wilfully fussy. My parents were definitely that hardline with me. 'Eat what you're given, Romesh, or you can starve.' But things are different now. The truth is, it's a lot more complicated to be a parent in the modern world, partly because we know so much more about our children. We know, for example, that some children are more sensitive than others to things like smell and noise, and that the way previous generations might have dealt with – or not recognized – these hypersensitivities would more than likely give those children hang-ups for the rest of their lives. My wife apparently hated peas and was forced by her school to eat every last one of them before she was allowed out to play. To this day she cannot bear them, to the point where even reading this would make her feel nauseous. Fortunately she takes so little interest in what I do that there's no chance of that happening.

Leesa sees her pea trauma as evidence that we should be

considerate and understanding of kids' fussiness, whereas I see it as evidence that it's her shitty genetics that have led to this problem with our own kids in the first place. Can you inherit a picky eating habit?

Other people are a problem too. Restaurants are competitive places for parents. You can guarantee that while your kids smash each other in the face with pizza slices, across at another table will be a family whose children are finishing their risotto, silently putting their cutlery down and exclaiming: 'Oh, Mummy! The seasoning in that was lovely!', and then they all laugh at how charming it is that their kid said something an adult would say, whereas in reality it's actually really creepy to hear a child say that, and if you did hear an adult say that you probably wouldn't want to hang out with them either. And then, in the middle of that thought, you are distracted by your glasses being knocked off your face by a bread roll, and you try to bollock your kids but you can't because your wife is almost pissing herself laughing. I imagine.

I occasionally become convinced that our kids behave like this to wind us up. We were on holiday in Dubai recently, which is a really nice place to go as long as you don't mind having a daily series of panic attacks about how much you're spending. We had dinner, then our kids asked us to buy them ice cream. I had, for some reason, decided that rather than just accept this holiday was going to be expensive, I would work out the price of each and every thing we were getting so my catchphrase for the holiday could be: 'I cannot fucking believe how much that costs.'

But much as I was balking at the expense, we were on

holiday, and obviously I told the kids they could have ice cream. I watched as they frolicked up to the lovely man at the counter and placed their order, deliberating over a selection of toppings that were arguably excessive. One of the kids came back with an ice cream that had three Snickers bars sticking out of the top. My only thought was at least that went some way towards clawing back the fortune each of those diabetes-inducers had cost us.

It was as much as I could do, however, not to hurl the ice cream across the room a few minutes later when, after eating some of the toppings and stirring the ice creams for a bit, they announced they were full. This time, there was no way the ice creams smelt funny or were not what they wanted – they were incredible. But not only had the kids decided they'd had enough, they'd done so much finger-licking and dipping into them that they had rendered them toxic to anyone else. Had they not done this, I might have contemplated abandoning my veganism to eat them just on financial principle. What ended up happening was that I decided to teach them a lesson about ordering things they didn't want. And that was how I found myself demanding the children finish what they had ordered. It's probably the first time Dubai's holiday-makers have seen children eating ice cream while crying.

In Portugal, after nugget-gate, I decided I was going to tackle this food issue actively. Before I became a parent, I had all these ideals about setting up expectations and making sure the children adhere to them so they grow up with a crystal-clear understanding of how to behave. In reality, what happens is that you take them out, they start pissing about, and you're so exhausted you think, 'Is it really such a big deal if they bite that dog?'

I was of the opinion that we had let the food thing slide, however, and I proudly told my wife I was taking action. She told me she was really glad to hear it. At the time I thought that was because she was excited to be inspired by what I was doing as a parent, but now I realize she was just excited about how much of a prick I was going to make of myself.

We sat down in a lovely restaurant and I made some subtle comments about how we should all think carefully about what we were ordering and maybe we should ask questions of the waiter to make sure we were getting what we really wanted. My wife nodded and agreed, I imagine trying to contain her joy at being able to see all of this go tits up.

One of the kids ordered a fish dish. Immediately alarm bells started ringing – this was going to be real fish. The fish our son likes is where they take whatever happens to fall off fish and compress it into fish shapes. I explained to him that this was going to be an actual fish, and he sternly informed me that he knew what fish was and that's what he wanted to eat. I said OK and explained that he would have to eat it.

This fish dish had now become my hill to die on. I knew I was going to have to make sure my son ate that fish so I could prove my point, educate the kids, but more importantly try to get some impressed holiday sex from my wife. I steeled myself for the challenge ahead. I looked at my son. He didn't realize it yet, but we were now locked in battle.

The fish arrived and it had skin on it. My wife nearly punched the air. She knew she was about to see something pretty special. My son took one look at the fish and said, 'Urr, skin, I can't eat this!' Almost exactly as he said this I glanced across the restaurant and saw a child who had ordered the same dish lifting the crispy skin and lowering it into his mouth like a hungry shark that was also a smug little shit.

I told my son that the fish looked great and he was going to eat it. He refused. He said it was disgusting. I explained to him that he was only saying that because he hadn't tried it and that if he wanted to, he would eat it, which is arguably one of the most pathetically circuitous arguments that anyone could come up with.

I insisted he try the fish. He agreed, taking a tiny speck of it, putting it into his mouth and informing me that it was the most disgusting thing he had ever eaten, which is weird because I once saw him eat a Quaver he found behind a car seat. (To be fair, I did the same when I found an Oreo once, and I found the staleness actually slightly improved it.) This was going badly, and I could tell how badly it was going because my wife was smiling.

My thinking was, if I could make him eat the fish, he would enjoy it, and then I would forever be able to tell him he was being silly every time he refused to eat anything. This was a very tricky moment, and I was starting to feel like the whole holiday hinged on it. I decided that my only option was to bribe him – he would accept the bribe, eat the fish, and his protests would be shattered for ever. He was due to get a PlayStation for his birthday, a fact that I find embarrassing even typing here. That gave me the idea.

Our children never seem grateful enough to me. That

might seem an odd statement straight after admitting that we were buying one of our sons a PlayStation for his birthday, but we really do try to make sure they value what they have. My parents, after initially spoiling us as young children, fell on hard times, so we were given an appreciation for things by accident rather than by design. In my head, I was always extremely grateful for what I was given, but that could be me looking back through rose-tinted glasses. I'm sure if you spoke to my late father, he'd tell you he didn't know why he bloody bothered.

Every generation thinks their kids are terribly behaved. Recently one of my kids was dancing with his penis out at breakfast and I looked at him to stop. He caught my eye, smiled, and if anything started gyrating with more vigour. I then told him to stop, before saying that in my day my parents would just have to look at me and I would stop misbehaving. Except that wasn't true – that was actually something my dad used to say to me about his childhood when I wouldn't stop messing about. So from that I can only assume he was a little prick too.

I don't think kids should be grateful by default because we as parents have done anything amazing for them – not at all. They don't owe us anything. I have been a long-term subscriber to the belief that since kids have no say about being brought into the world, the least you can do is make it as easy as possible for them to have the nicest life they can. Sometimes that means you buy them a PlayStation, and sometimes it doesn't. That choice is yours.

What I do think, though, is that kids should learn to be grateful for what they have, and they shouldn't be allowed to take anything for granted. Not least because when your kids are less than grateful for something they're given it's really embarrassing. I remember one Christmas having family round and watching one of our sons tear through the wrapping paper on his gifts, giving very honest appraisals about what exactly he thought of the presents, and helpfully informing people immediately if they had got him something he already had. We were mortified, while also silently furious with our family members who had not followed present instructions, which now meant we were going to have to go to the shops to exchange them.

I knew I needed a decent bribe to convince the kid to eat the fish and so I decided to go big. Looking across at my wife to make sure she was watching the masterclass, I told my son that I was so convinced he was not eating the fish just to be fussy, that I would buy him VR goggles to go with his PlayStation if he ate it. I had barely finished the sentence before I saw him dropping the skin into his mouth just like the kid from the other table. I was elated. I had made this boy eat fish skin – something I had never seen him do before. I looked across at my wife, who had an expression on her face that was more of disbelief than the sexually aroused admiration I had been hoping for.

It was about then that I realized what a complete and utter moron I had been. I had essentially paid my son £200 to eat some fish. Not only had I suggested to the child that if he wanted anything he could always try refusing to eat his dinner, but I had actually encouraged all of them to pretend they didn't like their food in the hope of getting some sort of payout, like tiny benefits cheats.

The rest of the holiday I occupied myself with undoing the lessons I had taught them that night. Every evening we would go to a restaurant and they would order something before asking me what they could have if they finished, and every night my face would receive a fresh application of egg.

I guess what I'm trying to say is I'm fucking clueless. I am in no way in a position to give you guidance about anything. But in this book I hope to explore the various issues we all encounter and give you some helpful and interesting thoughts on them. But absolutely do not take that to mean I am telling you what to do. Why would you take advice from someone who opens his book about life with an anecdote about paying his son to eat fish?

Sex

The relationship you have with sex changes as you get older. When you're a young man, it's all you can think about. You fantasize about how much you're going to get, and you think about how brilliant you're going to be at it when you do get it, visualizing mammoth sex sessions where whoever is on the receiving end lets all of their friends know how amazing you are in the sack and, before you know it, your scrotum looks like a pickled walnut because of all the jizzing you are doing.

After you've been married for a while, there are a number of possible outcomes – you might still be going at it on the regular with abandon and having those mammoth sessions, your passion not diluted one iota from when you first got together. To those people I would say, where do you find the time and energy? There are others of you who have accepted that it's a bit of an effort now, and have given up on that side of things altogether. To those people I would say, congratulations on coming to a conclusion that's going to bring you nothing but happiness. Most people fall into a third category, which is where you feel you have to be having sex because that's a sign of a healthy relationship, but it does feel like a bit of a commitment. In the past you might have cleared an evening, but now you try and fit it in early enough so you can watch two episodes of a box set before bed. I'm not going to say which group we fall into because that would be indiscreet but I will tell you that we are watching a lot of *Sneaky Pete* at the moment. When you are a decade into a marriage, sex is a bit like making a risotto – it's always nice, but a lot of the time you really can't be arsed.

I suppose there are some things you shouldn't divulge, or at least you should be vague about, or maybe even lie about. Perhaps I should be giving the impression that we visit Smashtown every evening, the neighbours concerned that we're fighting every night because it's so passionate, but the truth is there's very little chance we'll even wake the kids, unless their ears are particularly sensitive to a kind of exhausted wheezing, like a Labrador running uphill.

I talk a fair bit about sex on my latest stand-up tour, and people often ask Leesa if she is OK about how much I open up about our private life. There is a perverse nature to how I approach these things, as a lot of what I say on stage I wouldn't even have the guts to say to my very close friends. In fact, they have often found out about my true feelings from coming to watch me at gigs, usually without realizing I'm telling a story about them.

I don't have that luxury when talking about my sex life, though, as Leesa will have a pretty good inkling I'm talking about her. The truth is that of course I'm exaggerating for comic effect, but the sentiment is always based on truth. Sex is such a taboo. That sounds insane when you think about how readily available pornography is, but I don't mean sexual content, I mean the sexual dynamics of relationships. People find it so uncomfortable to talk about.

Children obviously have their part to play in our case. It's very difficult to be unexhausted enough to engage in passionate sex, plus we have both discussed the horror of one of them walking in on us. I don't even know how much money would have to go into counselling the boys out of 'that time we were at Butlin's and I saw my dad's flat arse going up and down at what even as a child I would describe as quite a sedate pace'. I don't know if I could bear the children walking in. Some of my friends have stories of walking in on their parents when they were younger and they are still scarred. I remember our parents taking us to a hotel for the weekend and then, weirdly, just locking us out of their bedroom. My brother and I started singing a very loud song about how bored we were, though we might as well have improvised a number called 'Boner Killer'. My mum really won't want me telling that story, so I would appreciate it if we could keep it from her. She's never going to read this, and if she does, Mum, why would you read a chapter your son has written about sex, you weirdo?

Leesa and I are, I think, more worried about whether our sex life is an indictment of our relationship than anything else. We do enjoy the, you know, sexy time, but life and children make it very difficult. It's also pretty tricky to know how to refer to it, so bringing up a lack of action can be an issue in itself. You don't have to refer to it in the early days, because you're doing it so much that it doesn't need talking about. You wake up and you do it, you go to bed and do it, and sometimes if you're my parents you lock the bedroom door to keep people out and do it. When you're in a comfortable relationship you might be discussing the possibility of scheduling some time in for it next week. Then it becomes tricky to know how to label it. 'Sex' sounds too clinical, but the problem is all the nicknames sound too funny when said in an adult conversation about diary arrangements. 'Next Thursday after dinner do you fancy a shag/fuck/bonk/fornicate/doing it/hump/knee trembler/pump/bang bang/hello sailor. I don't know, it may be the level of maturity of the words I'm using that's the problem.

I've forgotten what it's like when you don't have kids. At least with kids you have some sort of excuse – you can say, 'Oh, I think I heard one of them say something' if you're not up for it. If Leesa says that to me, she knows it will be at least an hour and a half before any blood will travel to my penis, and I am happy with that buffer. If you don't have kids, what do you do? Are people without kids shagging all the time simply because they don't have a convenient get-out? I am not saying that sex is not fun, of course it is. But similarly Chessington World of Adventures is fun but I wouldn't want to go every day. I say all this as if I'm the one constantly knocking it back. The truth is, Leesa is the one who has to stand me down, so to speak. Both on sex and going to Chessington.

Sometimes she suspects I'm going to suggest sex and

gets an excuse in early, usually after we finish dinner. She will say something like, 'That was really filling, wasn't it?' and what she means is – 'Do not even think of trying to touch me later.' Or we might go upstairs and she starts taking her clothes off in a very nonsexual way, saying things like, 'I'm so hot.' Now, to be fair, that sounds like the beginning of soft porn, but it's the manner in which she does it. She says she's hot like she's a frustrated toddler, and she pulls the clothes off in a manner that suggests they're drenched in sweat. These are all signs for me to put away the launch codes because it's not happening that night.

I have joked in the past about me thinking this is insensitive, but the truth is this poor woman is trying to protect me. She should just be able to say, 'I don't fancy it tonight, Rom. Maybe think about the kind of shape you're in to up the chances, eh?' Instead, she has to enter into some sort of exhausted/bloated/flustered role play where she doesn't have to actually reject me.

While we are on the subject of turn-offs – and before I say this I'd like to point out that I am fully aware that men have it so much easier than women when it comes to body image, and I'm sure that people will tell me I'm self-body-shaming and all of that – but honestly, my physique is too funny to be sexy. It really is. I know that for a fact because it looks funny when I'm just standing up. If you want proof of that, take a look at the Stormzy performance Jamie Redknapp and I did on *A League Of Their Own*. People have told me how funny that was. How was it funny? I don't mean to get all Joe Pesci about it, but all I did was rap with my top off. So what people are actually saying is that my body makes them laugh, and I don't think that's a compliment.

It's for this reason that I kind of pity Leesa for having to deal with it. She must be thinking the whole time: 'Must keep a straight face, must keep a straight face.' It's a credit to the wonderful heart of that woman that she manages it most of the time. The reality of sex is so innately hilarious, though. You have to do these really intense faces, and while in films and porn they always switch into new brilliant positions, in reality you rarely hit comfort straight away. I would love porn to include more of the bits where one of them says, 'Yeah that's really good, but can you move over that way a bit, because I'm in quite a lot of pain.'

You do start to worry about what not having sex means for your relationship, though. I've read countless articles that suggest the first sign a marriage is struggling is when the sex slows down, and whenever you read about people having affairs it's because their partner wasn't showing them attention and providing them with what they need or whatever.

I once jokingly asked Leesa about this and she replied that living with the boys and me left her too tired to think about anything like that. And I'm pretty happy about that. If you want to keep your relationship together, you either show them the love and attention they need so they can live a happy life and never think about going elsewhere, or you can drain them physically and emotionally to the point where trying to go and search for something better would be just too exhausting.

We have actually decided to be a lot more chilled out about it, which I think is helpful. Rather than panicking about the fact we haven't docked for a bit, we just live our lives and then, when it does happen, it's a lovely surprise that doesn't feel like putting the bins out. Can't wait till we get round to it again in about six months.

Friendship

My male friends are the same group of people I have hung out with since I was a kid, and I think that's the case for a lot of men, despite the fact that it does undermine the whole concept a little bit. How the hell can I at forty-two still be good friends with someone I first met when I was ten? If you're telling me there hasn't been any kind of 'you'll do' thinking there, I'd find it hard to believe.

Our friendships have evolved over the years, and I think that's partly because of getting closer through time, and partly because men have become better at talking to each other about their issues, as those stereotypes about men failing to acknowledge and discuss their feelings have been eroded.

This isn't the case when men are in groups, though. A bunch of men in a pub collectively form the most disgustingly uncivilized pack of animals you could hope to encounter. They are lewd and shouty and as soon as they spot a weakness in any member of their group, they will turn on them and attack mercilessly, each one of them simultaneously relieved that they aren't the one that's the target. I have been on nights out with friends where, if one of the group is perceived to be going to the toilet too much, he is outed and verbally flogged with the kind of venom you'd reserve for a sex offender.

It does mellow as you get older, but things that happened twenty years ago can still be brought up at any moment. For example, at the end of the 1990s, a friend of ours was entertaining the group by impersonating our dancing. During the process, he managed to stumble and fall. We all laughed hysterically, and he waited for us to finish before informing us that he had actually hurt his ankle quite badly and would have to go to A&E. He has had to spend the rest of his life being reminded of that every time he comes out. 'Anyone want a drink? Not you, mate, we know what you're like! Hahahahahahaaa!' It's the gift that kept on giving. Another friend knocked a girl back who everyone else thought was attractive – he was called homosexual for a solid five years after that.

There is something about men that means they have to engage with each other like that when en masse. I don't want to suggest I'm above it, either. I'm happy to savage anyone who expresses a view that differs from the group's collective opinion. What's that? You thought *Iron Man 2* was good? Oi, lads, look at this little *Iron Man 2*-loving piece of shit! I cannot believe you liked that film, you absolute muggy little cunt! I bet you loved Whiplash, didn't you? Your favourite villain – you dick! Next he'll be saying he enjoyed *Age of Ultron*, the absolute wanker.

Individually, however, men are completely different. I would happily go to any of my friends with any of my problems in a heartbeat, and I know that they would do everything they could to help me. Weirdly, if I told any one of them individually something embarrassing, it would never be on the table for banter. I could tell a friend that I had a desperate fear of nipples and it was messing me up, and it wouldn't get mentioned again, but if I alluded to it on a night out, the rest of the evening would be them coming up with horror film titles that had the word 'nipple' in. (Mine would be *The (Nipple) Ring*. It's actually quite hard to do this.)

As the years have gone by, we've moved through the gears of evenings out, but arguably not quickly enough. Once you're in your late thirties and forties, I would argue that you're actually being quite selfish going out to the same places that younger people are going to because you are reminding them of their possible future. Or, conversely, providing a warning to them of the dangers of what happens if you don't accept you're getting older. We have started to go to restaurants and crazy golf, and things that can give us the illusion of having an evening that isn't just roast whoever you can, get drunk, take it too far, feel awful about it the next day. The fact that I've been spending more of these nights sober has also meant we needed to bring another form of structure to the occasion.

That's the other thing about nights out with our friends now. There was a time when nothing would get in the way. You would cancel things to make it for even a part of the evening. You would get smashed and go straight into work the next day. Now, I have known people to pull out of a get-together because they found out the parking is a nightmare, or because they suddenly felt quite tired. As a cancel addict myself, I never judge these people, but I have been on the other side of a night out for ten being whittled down to two on the day.

There is also the prospect of going to friends' houses that increasingly gets thrown into the mix once children come along and people can afford more than one chair. I would happily advocate a complete ban on this. Going to people's houses and having people over is truly fucking awful. When I go to somebody's house I immediately feel like a prisoner. I feel like I've visited a rival gang boss on their territory and will only be allowed to leave when they say so. I also find using other people's toilets absolutely terrifying. On the one hand, the toilets could be disgusting and you have to try not to touch anything. On the other hand, the toilets might be biological-level clean and I panic that I'm going to accidentally piss everywhere. I always sit down to piss at someone else's house. You have to. It's not worth the dice roll.

The other rule is that under no circumstances do you shit in another person's house. If you are an overnight guest, then fine, but only if completely necessary and you scrub that bowl afterwards. I don't know why I feel so strongly about this, but I do. Psychologically, when I go to somebody's house, I just completely decommission my arsehole for the evening. I help this process by eating absolutely nothing during the day in the lead-up to the visit, which enables me to be confident that when I do go to the toilet and sit down for a wazz, I do not suddenly activate a different sequence. If I'm at someone's house and I need to go, I will either tell them I have to leave, if I know them well enough, or, if I don't, I'll pretend I'm ill or something. Genuinely. I just can't.

I find friendship a difficult thing to get my head around. As I've got older, I've decided I'm off the market for new friends. I might meet up with people, usually at Leesa's insistence, but only so I still have an eye on the game. I suppose if I end up really getting on with someone then I can replace that idiot who liked *Iron Man 2*.

The reason I question friendship is that I think it's very easy to feel lonely as a bloke. I don't have a circle of friends I lean on or share things with – even though I know I could, I don't – but that might just be particular to my friends. I see Leesa and her friends talking through their problems and helping each other out and it's like a proper support network. Instead, I have a group of people I can go out with. I realize this contradicts my assertion that we would do anything for each other. That is true, but on the other hand I don't know if any of us would ever ask if someone else was all right.

I'm making this seem like I feel all sad about my friendships – I don't. I think I have a great group of friends whom I'm lucky to have, bar the one I'm trying to replace. It's just that it's easy to fall into a situation where you are meeting up with the boys to talk football and bullshit, and unless you really make an effort to move conversations beyond that and take a real interest in what your friends are up to and what's going on in their lives, then you run the risk of those relationships becoming trivial. It's the same as with your partner. You can fall into the trap of all your conversations being functional and about what you have to do that week, and it's only when you actively look to have a real chat that you have a proper conversation, like about how horrible the toilets were at that dinner party.

I sound like I'm being all guruish here and I apologize for that, but it is something that really bothers me. You can have friends and family around you but still feel incredibly lonely. I think men need to be better at having those honest and exposing conversations that form proper connections.

The reason I have come over all pontifical is that I had a conversation like this with a friend recently. He had started to get incredibly stressed out about a series of things that had happened to him, and he knew I had used therapy in the past. He wanted to know if I could recommend anyone for him to see. He's an extremely good friend of mine, and I have a lot of affection for him, but it was in that moment that I realized I wasn't best equipped to have this conversation with him because we had so rarely talked about things in this way. Our chats were usually joke-filled descriptions of how various things had pissed us off, checking if we were OK at work, talking about how shit Arsenal are and so on. None of this has felt like small talk. I very much enjoy hanging out with the bloke, but it became apparent to me that we didn't have, or at least hadn't had, many real conversations about feelings and struggles and worries. It seems crazy, doesn't it – because those things tend to be what occupy your thoughts the most and yet, in the case of a lot of men at least, we find them the most difficult things to openly discuss.

I asked my friend what had caused him to feel this way and he completely opened up, explaining the stresses he had been under at work and how they had been building up, leading to the point where he couldn't take it any more and needed help because he wasn't coping. It was genuinely a good conversation, although there is something of the grief vampire in me talking so enthusiastically about him going through a shit ton of stress. It was, however, great to be able to give him some genuine support and talk to him about it all, and I was happy he felt he could open up to me.

Now, I'm not telling this story because I'm some remarkable friend therapist or even to suggest that I helped solve the guy's problems, but it's an event that made me think about why we need friends around us in the first place. Yes, so you can socialize and rip the piss out of each other, that's all important in its own way, but it's just as vital to have people you can turn to when shit hits fan. Or, frankly, as soon as the fan gets turned on. Men often leave it too late to reach out for help, bottling things up until the pressure becomes unbearable. Why? Talking about things can help us work through them.

If my mate hadn't told me I'd have had no idea he was struggling. That phone call reinforced my belief that it's important for us to properly check in with each other when we are talking, rather than just going over the usual superficial subjects. It's one thing to humiliate your friends in public, but try to make sure that in private you're looking out for them too.

Flake

Having said all this about friendship, the text message I probably send the most to people is an apology for cancelling a night out or an apology for not getting in touch to reorganize the night out as I promised I would. Then there's the text apology for not texting them at all. There are a good number of people who have given up on texting me or asking me to go out, and I'm pretty certain I'm amassing a group of ex-friends who think I'm an inconsiderate prick.

I became convinced for a while that I had a condition that has been dubbed 'cancellation ecstasy'. I love cancelling. It's glorious. You have arranged to go out for dinner or a night at the pub, and as the time approaches you start to dread getting ready and leaving the house. You start thinking it feels more hassle than it's worth, and then you start to resent the fact you are having to go out at all. A few hours before the event, you convince yourself that the right thing to do for your mental health is to not go out at all, and you cancel, actually feeling noble because you are taking steps to protect yourself. Normally, as I come to this acceptance so late in proceedings, I have to make up something pretty extreme to get out of it – a text message saying something like, 'This is Romesh's wife – he's dead and so won't be able to make it tonight.'

A few months ago, I was completely swamped with work stuff, and I received a voicemail from Bobo, the man who was my guide in the Sahara episode of *The Misadventures of Romesh Ranganathan* and someone I have a lot of time for. He told me he was doing a trip across Europe, and would be spending a small amount of time in London and would love to meet up. All of this is made more incredible by the fact that Bobo cannot read and relies on the kindness of strangers to help him make planes and public transport. Apparently he has never missed anything and always manages to find his way, and I'm staggered that he does this, bearing in mind that in Britain I'm pretty sure many people would wilfully give him the wrong information for shits and giggles.

I heard the voicemail, got excited about seeing him, put the phone back in my pocket and promptly forgot all about it. He then sent me another voicemail, which I listened to, thought, 'Oh God, I must get in touch with him', before putting my phone away and completely forgetting about it again. I then received a third voicemail, this time from the family Bobo was staying with in London, saying he'd arrived and had been trying to get hold of me, and that he was worried he wasn't going to see me while in the UK. I felt like such a massive prick. I had been so ignorant I had managed to potentially upset a man I have nothing but affection for. It's a weird contradiction, because I like him a lot and was keen to see him, but to all intents and purposes it looked like I was trying to avoid him.

I got in touch with Bobo immediately and arranged to see him. He asked me where to meet, I told him the name of the bar, and was about to give him the address when he told me he needed no further details. I have no idea how this man navigates anywhere but I did consider changing the location to the most obscure place I could possibly think of just to see how good he really is.

It was an absolute delight to see Bobo. He is a truly wonderful man, and I loved catching up with him and mainly telling him how mad I thought it was that he could travel around Europe without being able to read. He must get annoyed about it, in the same way that I do about being asked how I manage to remain so overweight despite being a vegan, but that didn't stop me telling him over and over again.

We popped outside for Bobo to have a cigarette (and I definitely didn't have a cigarette as I'm a non-smoker on my life insurance and would never be that stupid), when a girl walked past, took one look at the both of us, said she had loved the Sahara show and immediately started crying. She explained that it was her birthday and everything had gone wrong and she was having the worst day ever. Bobo immediately undid one of his bracelets and gave it to her, saying, 'This is from me for your birthday.' Two things struck me at that moment – what an incredible man Bobo was for doing that and what a kind heart he must have, but also how it made me look like a right arsehole by comparison. I did wish her a Happy Birthday but that felt pretty worthless at this point and I'm pretty sure she was eyeing up my watch.

I loved spending that time with Bobo, although it was tainted by the fact that I had come across so badly in the run-up to it. It did make me think that I should make more of an effort to meet up with people when it's first been suggested, rather than, as I usually do, waiting until I feel like I have to avoid pissing them off by cancelling for the fifth consecutive time.

I talked about my flakiness on stage recently, and a few friends heard about the routine and then texted me to cite incidents where I'd cancelled and made up an excuse that I had now retrospectively revealed was bullshit. I contemplated texting them back to deny I had been talking about an occasion involving them, but then I realized I might have been given a gift. If everyone knows your excuses are nonsense, you don't need to make them. Perhaps I could now just text, 'Sorry, feeling flaky so I'm not coming.' That would be refreshing. But I suspect that level of inconsiderateness would lead to me just not being invited to anything any more, which would be a shame, because having nothing to do is nowhere near as good as planning to have something to do and then getting out of it. I'd miss that euphoria.

I'm trying to stop the last-minute-cancellation thing, though it does put a bit of pressure on the evening. I might be out with friends, the conversation dries up and I think, 'I definitely should have cancelled this.' From now on, however, if I ever cancel anything, it's for genuine reasons. And those reasons might include the fact I really don't feel like it any more. Just don't you dare try cancellling on me.

Holidays

Holidays are what keep you clinging to the idea there is some sort of point to the work–retire–die cycle we have convinced ourselves is life. They are moments of freedom and purpose. In adulthood, you fall into a pattern of going through the daily grind of work desperately looking forward to the next break you have booked, hoping beyond hope that it will offset the misery of having to be somewhere every day that is slowly draining the life out of you.

Even if you're lucky enough to be doing a job you love, chances are you spend so much time doing it that you barely see your friends and family. You come home one day, turn to your other half and say, 'Shall we book somewhere nice to go to?' And what you actually mean is, 'If we don't book a holiday I'm going to start wondering why the fuck I work at all and I'm probably going to start drinking myself to death.'

And that's exactly what a holiday is. If you're going to have an existential crisis about why exactly it is we feel the need to get on the property ladder, have children, burden ourselves with debt and work ourselves to the bone until we're sixty-five or dead, all because we need to maintain an illusion of purpose, you might as well have it somewhere sunny.

I want my holidays to be boring, in the best possible way. I want to find the familiar spots, I want to find the best places to eat, and then rinse and repeat for two weeks, with the occasional spontaneous bit of crazy golf.

There are certain parts of a holiday you have to do for the children and which no self-respecting adult enjoys. You would have to declare yourself an absolute prick of a parent to not take your kids to the waterpark. The water-park is the most disgusting cesspit of an idea, which I cannot believe still exists, and hopefully will be abolished after coronavirus makes everyone realize that we should limit sharing secretions. Five minutes watching the kids' pool area is enough to ascertain that most of that blue water is a cocktail of snot and saliva, plus whatever is coming off and out of people's bodies by way of skin, urine, and whatever dirt they happen to carry. I mean, it is fucking rank, and as I'm typing this I am contemplating starting a campaign to have them shut down.

I wouldn't mind the lows of a waterpark being so lethally low if the highs were good, but they're shit too. Waterslides are fucking awful. My wife always says I'm smiling when I come out, but I think that might be the euphoria that it's over and I'm not paralysed and don't appear to have picked up AIDS. The AIDS fear is a random one, I grant you, but when I was a kid everyone said that people put infected needles in the waterslides and I have never been able to shake that idea off. And based on the level of genital soak-age that goes on all day, with the same water being pumped round and round, I think it's pretty likely you're going to get everything that's going just by being there.

You queue up for a waterslide for absolutely ages in your bathing suit. Awful. It's one thing to be in swim shorts by the pool, but I can't stand and have a casual chat with someone with my body exposed like that, while standing behind a European man with a body fat percentage of 'Your wife can't stop looking at me'. On top of that, nobody is wearing anything and I don't want to look like a pervert, not easy when your eyes are not completely under your control, and so I spend the whole time looking at the ground, with my kids wondering what's going on. It's when looking at the ground that I notice I haven't cut my toenails recently, and that's another thing to feel paranoid about. Can we also all agree that the slides are not actually that much fun? You spend ages waiting for your turn, then endure about 15 seconds of mild agony as a series of ridges dig you in the back before you splash down in the least dignified way possible.

I realize I sound like a grinch here, but let me say this: fuck waterparks. Or at least that's what I would say if not for the fact that I've never seen a day out make my kids happier. They love it. We arrive at the park, and they're sprinting to find a spot to leave our things before wanting to hit up every single slide as quickly as possible, undaunted by the fact that the whole day is a ratio of five hours' queuing to about a minute and a half of actual 'fun'. I cannot be the guy who stops them having a day on their holiday like that and, actually, I hate to admit it but you end up enjoying it purely because the kids are buzzing their little tits off. Then you remember you've probably ingested about half a pint of snot.

There are times when you convince yourself something has been more magical than it was. We had talked about going to Disneyland for years and eventually decided we'd try out the one in Paris to see what the boys thought. Because I wanted it to be super-special, I forked out for the top package where you stay at the hotel and Mickey Mouse gives you a hand job after dinner.

When we arrived, the guy at reception asked for my name and saw that I had booked some premium thing and said, 'You are about to have the most magical time ever, sir!'

It was pretty sick. The room had chocolates hidden all around it and we had an exclusive lift that took us to the door of the park. We also had this dining experience where the characters would come round and sign an autograph book, which is an absolutely perfect example of a resort making something seem desirable. At the end of our time there, each of our children had a book full of underpaid teenagers' signatures.

The big problem was that it pissed it down with rain for the entire time, and there is just no getting around that as a literal dampener. Every time we queued for a ride we would then have to find somewhere to dry the boys off. Even they were starting to feel the gloss was coming off Mickey a bit. We struggled on, mainly driven by my desire not to have the exorbitant amount of money I had spent go to waste. It's an awful feeling that, isn't it? Where you have spent so much money you feel like you are on high stress the entire time. You try to be casual about how much breakfast cost, even though you know you are being absolutely shafted. It was Dubai all over again. Part of it comes from worrying the boys might think this sort of thing is usual. I keep having to reiterate to them how costly it all is, hoping it will teach them to value things, but in reality it just ruins the holiday for everybody.

At the end of the trip, we decided to get the boys pancakes and go and watch the nightly firework display. We set up in a good position, after moving a couple of times because of inconsiderate families setting up in front of us. It's so funny to me how tribalistic we all get in situations like this – every other family representing a group of people we are competing with to get the best experience. If anyone pisses you off, you communicate your anger through loud conversation with each other:

'Yes, well, I suppose we will have to move as this family here don't seem to care if other people can see or not.'

'Yes, kids, I know you want to see the castle, but these people are obviously cunts.'

Once we had established our position, we sat and watched the display. Halfway through, I looked across at the children and they were in complete and utter awe at what they were seeing. Their faces were textbook 'children in wonder', eyes wide, mouths open. I felt like I was going to cry a little bit. I wondered if I'd been bitten by the magic of Disney, but realized it was much more likely that I was tired, drenched and regretting the amount of money we had spent to be here.

What all of this does is put an incredible amount of pressure on your break. Whether you're spending a fortune to keep your kids quiet at Disneyland or picking up verrucas in a Spanish waterpark, holidays come laden with expectation. You start visualizing that trip as the reset button where you can have quality time with your family, you're going to eat beautiful food and you're going to watch the sunset. Unsurprisingly, holidays rarely live up to the hype.

Something I am exceptional at is doing things regardless of the consequences and then becoming embittered when the consequences bite me in the penis. I would say bite me in the arse, but I wilfully cause myself major issues regularly and they're far more painful. It's like I have a person inside me trying to screw me over at every opportunity. I really relate to the Nutty Professor, and not just because I look a little bit like Sherman Klump.

Take the Dubai holiday. I was getting some tattoo bits done just before I went. Our hotel was attached to a waterpark so I was excited about every day being a viral-infection dice roll. During the tattooing, the artist said to me, 'So what are you up to?' and I had excitedly told her about my holiday. It was at this point that she reminded me you have to keep a new tattoo out of the sun and out of the water for about three weeks.

My immediate internal reaction was, 'FUCKING HELL I KNEW THIS WHY THE FUCK AM I GETTING A TATTOO I AM SUCH A FUCKING ABSOLUTE PRICK!' All I said, however, was, 'Yep, of course, I'll be careful.'

I went home to break the news to Leesa and the kids, ready to be unreasonably annoyed with Leesa for not telling me I shouldn't get new tattoos just before a holiday.

Leesa was, understandably, in disbelief. Why on earth would someone who doesn't need to get tattoos ever suddenly decide to get one that would ruin the trip? It was incredible work by me.

I promised my family I would find a solution. For a while I dabbled with the idea of ignoring the advice and having the tattoo redone if needs be, until I read stories of people getting new tattoos, going swimming in a public pool and then having to have their leg amputated. I decided against that, even though it would have given me some good stand-up material.

After an hour or so of internet hunting, I found what I felt could be a viable solution – a waterproof rubber limb sock. It was for people who had to keep casts dry, because there is no way you would design a product for the small market of people stupid enough to get a tattoo the day before they were due to stay at a waterpark.

I ordered the arm sock and waited for the family to display their excitement. It arrived and I unwrapped it to try it on and show my family how I'd found a way to fully engage with the holiday. There were two issues. One, it was designed to go over a cast and be waterproof, so it had to be tight, and comfort wasn't an issue because it would be pushing against a cast. As soon as I put it on my bare, recently inked arm, it felt like I was wearing a tourniquet. I was in agony. This feeling didn't subside with time spent wearing the thing, despite my arm slowly going numb. No matter, it was a solution.

The other issue was that I looked like an absolute prick. It was bright blue, went right up my arm and looked like an oven glove. It was more embarrassing than I ever could have imagined. This was fine for me, as I was getting what I deserved, but slightly unfair on my family who, through no fault of their own, were going to spend their holiday walking around in forty-degree heat with a bell-end wearing a glove to protect the plaster cast he most definitely didn't have on underneath it.

When we got to Dubai, we spent the first afternoon looking for something that we could buy that would help me disguise the monstrosity, which also made me incredibly popular with the kids. We eventually found a hotel-branded wetsuit top that we thought would at least cover up the majority of the arm condom.

The first visit to the waterpark arrived and I got myself costumed up in front of my family, who had decided they were going to pretend it didn't look that bad, as much for their own mental health as for mine.

What I hadn't anticipated was the number of tourists there were going to be, which, bearing in mind I was on holiday, seems naive in the extreme. I had a weird experience in the queue for breakfast when an Indian man walked past me, stopped and turned to me and lost his shit – like when Prince Akeem is in that queue for the toilets in *Coming to America*. It sounds a bit bratty of me to say that, but he'd seen one of my travel shows on an Indian channel and I think it was more disbelief on his part than anything else.

At the waterpark, everyone who has ever watched my comedy was there. I got approached ten times within the first hour, and each time had to explain what I'd done to my arm. Even if it looked like they weren't going to ask, I thought it better to explain myself than have them tell their friends that I like to wear a limb johnny on holiday.

In the end, what happened was that I found it hellish and the kids found it hilarious – they actually started to enjoy how much of a terrible time I was having, as if they felt it was just punishment for what had happened.

I guess the message of all of this is that while holidays can be lovely, a lot of the time they can be angst-ridden. But when you are in the middle of a holiday nightmare or you're freaking out about how much money you're spending, you can always console yourself with the knowledge that this is as good as it gets and you'll be going back to work soon.

Politeness

Just before I go on tour, I always ask my agent to book the warm-up tour in the most far-flung parts of the UK. This is partly because the audiences can often be kinder, but mainly because I would hate to start the tour and then realize that none of the material works anywhere apart from West Sussex. I don't want to be in Scotland and hear one of them shout: 'We don't have a Shakeaway in Glasgow, you English bastard!'

My tour manager, Grazio, accompanied me to the Lake District for a number of the gigs ahead of my Cynic's Mixtape tour. Grazio is one of my favourite people in the world, which is handy. You spend so much time together on the road, exhausted, that if you didn't really get on somebody would wind up dead, most likely me because I reckon Graz can handle himself. My children now associate Graz with me going away for a bit and get upset when they see him, whereas Leesa is fucking delighted.

We had just finished a gig and headed to a beautiful hotel where we would indulge in what had become our post-gig usual – a rum and coke. We arrived at the hotel to find one poor bastard working reception through the night, waiting to check us in as the day's last arrivals. We asked if we could get a drink, and he then had to walk us to the bar to serve us. I often feel guilty about asking late-night hotel staff for a drink, usually after they've shut up the bar and assumed their guests are all done for the night. To be clear, I'm talking a low-level guilt that I feel relieved to unburden myself of now, but not enough guilt to actually stop me and Graz asking for a drink in every venue we stay at. The man asked us what we want and we requested our standard, and off he went to make them.

We were talking for a while when it occurred to us that the man was taking a long time to make the drinks. We weren't annoyed as much as we were utterly baffled because we were the only people in the bar and the bar itself was about 5 metres away from where we were sat. I looked over to see him looking around the shelves in what I would describe as a state of high stress. Immediately I felt for the guy, because if I was working through the night and two pricks had insisted on rum and coke I would have looked for approximately ten seconds before telling them that we didn't have it. This guy obviously had a level of dedication to his job that I'd never fully understand, and which meant that he took his whole rum and coke mission rather seriously. What added to the confusion, however, was that there was clearly a selection of rums behind him, as well as a full range of soft drinks at his disposal.

We didn't want to embarrass him, so we made the decision to wait it out. After another few minutes, the man returned to us empty-handed, looking a bit upset. He said, 'I'm really sorry, guys. I have looked absolutely everywhere and I cannot find any rummuka anywhere.' It became immediately clear that this man had spent the best part of ten minutes looking for a drink that he had never heard of, because he had just that second made it up. We clarified to him what we had actually ordered and off he went. When he returned with the drinks we were still pissing ourselves laughing and thanked him.

I felt bad about this, because I didn't want the man to think we were taking the piss out of him. It was just a funny misunderstanding. But I became really paranoid about offending him, both because he had been so nice to us and also because I'm not a total prick. The guy has a tough job and the last thing he needs is two people arriving late at night and behaving like wankers. We ended up giving him a huge tip because we felt so bad, but then after I went to bed it occurred to me that the whole thing might have been just his way of getting our sympathy. I imagined returning to the bar the next night to find him looking confused and saying to a customer: 'I am very sorry, but I cannot find any rodka.'

Late at night in hotels is often where you can see rank drunkenness. I think I have seen more rude, obnoxious encounters at a late-night hotel bar than I have in any other context, probably because when I am on tour that is where I do most of my drinking. There is something about the late-night alcohol combined with the fact that you are away from home and drinking in the same building you are going to sleep in that completes the prick conversion. I have been in a bar and seen a man screaming at a member of staff because he was under the impression that if he was staying at the hotel, they were legally obliged to keep serving him drinks until he decided he was finished. I saw a group of lads playing football in a bar, and telling the bar staff to fuck off when asked to stop. I probably should have intervened, but I'm the sort of guy who lets a barman look for a made-up drink for ten minutes without helping him.

I am always concerned about how I treat people in the service industry. To me it is one of the ultimate indicators of character. It is why so frequently when you are watching a film or a TV show, they convey that somebody is a bad person by showing them being a prick to a waiter or a shop assistant. It's a cliché but one that holds true because you are talking to someone who has, to a limit, no choice but to be nice to you regardless of your behaviour, because they are paid to be attentive and cheery. And so in customers you see how someone behaves when there is zero at stake, when there are no consequences to their level of rudeness. There is also a belief that, because you are paying for a service, that means you no longer have to talk to people like they're people. It is an incredible arsehole indicator.

I have on occasion experienced it myself. I sometimes do corporate gigs, which are a great way to make decent money in exchange for setting fire to your soul and presenting a few awards. Most of the time it's fine and the people get you in to do the job, watch you die on your arse pretending to give a shit about the South East Letting Agents awards, and then you go, but occasionally people genuinely treat you like they have bought you for the evening, taking you round to mingle with their friends and ordering you to be in photos with them. This is at least understandable to a degree as they are paying decent money.

What I don't understand is people who think it's OK to be rude to some poor fucker who works at Nando's.

I have gone off at friends because of the way they have spoken to service staff, mainly because I then worry that I have chosen to be friends with an arsehole. I would genuinely go so far as to say that I have seen the way people have spoken to service staff and thought, 'I am never going to hang out with you again.' Unless it's a really good mate I have no desire to correct their behaviour as I want their shittiness to remain apparent like a twat beacon for anyone else who thinks they might want to be friends with them.

I say all this, and then I think of all the times I have been a prick to service staff, which in isolation would make me look like the sort of person I myself would secretly cancel on, and then I realize it's not useful to be as binary about it as that.

I remember on one occasion, in my more hot-headed days, my girlfriend at the time had bought a coat for her brother from a sports shop in Kingston. When he tried it on, it hadn't fit and so we took it back to change it. The manager at the store said he didn't have any others, but if we kept hold of it, he would call us when the next one came in. When, after a week, we hadn't received a call my girlfriend got angry about it, and I'm ashamed to say that, in some sort of attempt to try and impress her, I decided I was going to be angry on her behalf. I walked into the store and started demanding answers from the manager, hoping that I was demonstrating enough rage to secure me some sort of blow-job reward later. The manager, slightly affronted at being spoken to like that by a teenager, essentially lost his temper and started being really rude in return. It turned out they had made a cock-up and not contacted us when the coat was back in stock, but I guess he saw my behaviour as a way of deflecting the blame, that I was now the one at fault. He sorted the coat out, while telling me how out of line I was and that they didn't want me in the store again. I was gobsmacked and probably a little wrongfooted, but being shocked was not going to impress my girlfriend and so I doubled down, getting even more outraged. The manager gave me the new coat, and as I walked out one of the members of staff smirked at me. In my excitement at securing the coat I turned to him to ask him what he was looking at.

In what I would then describe as possibly the maddest retail experience of my life, he told me to fuck off before following me out of the store alongside most of the team at the shop. I was then essentially stood outside Kingston JD Sports with my girlfriend facing off with most of the staff. It was incredible. The manager even came out. I don't know what kind of rogue store this was, but they were baying for blood, with the manager saying, 'Look what you've done now!' I have to admit, at this stage I was starting to worry more about getting an arse-kicking than looking like a hero, so I backed down and walked away, still in utter disbelief. Our only consolation was that when we got home we discovered they had forgotten to take the original coat and so we had got an inadvertent bogof. I tried to style out the whole episode to my girlfriend, pointing out that I'd backed down because we'd got the coat.

She went on to cheat on me several times after that and I often wonder if it was my conduct in the Bentall Centre that convinced her I was not the one. That was obviously an insane situation, but it did make me reflect on how I spoke to people who worked in shops. If anything, those staff at JD Sports did me a favour.

I would say that there are limits to this, and there are times when rage at service staff is reasonable. Around the same time as the JD Sports episode, I spent a long time working at Sunglass Hut in Gatwick Airport. A woman came in with a pair of sunglasses from which the arm had come off. She had no receipt, but we said we would try to fix them for her. Under the counter there was a box of glasses screws, so I selected the correct one and began to attempt the repair as my colleague watched. Unfortunately, the size of the screw, the thickness of the arm and the fatness of my fingers meant that it was extremely difficult to put the screw into place. I tried once, dropped and lost the screw, tried again with another and did the same. By the time I got to the fourth screw, all with the customer watching over me, myself and the other guy working there started getting the giggles, which made an already tricky task absolutely impossible. This poor woman had to watch me fail to fix her glasses, all the while finding it hilarious. I then asked my colleague if he could have a go, and he proceeded to fumble around in exactly the same way. This led to more laughter and lost screws. Eventually it got to the point where we realized that we just couldn't do it and we apologized to the customer. Understandably, she exploded. She went into a rant about how disgusting it was that we had not only not fixed them, but found that amusing, and she demanded the contact details for Head Office. It was deeply unpleasant to be on the receiving end of her tirade, but the whole time she went off I was thinking, 'This is absolutely what I deserve.' When I was next in with my manager, she pointed out that I could have exchanged the glasses and saved everyone a lot of trouble. If that woman happens to be reading this, I'm very sorry. I hope you enjoyed the new glasses you received as a direct result of my incompetence.

So I guess the point I am trying to make is, be polite to people unless they really don't deserve it.

Quality Time

My anxiety about not spending enough time with my children is ever-present and frightening. It's also undermined by the fact that I become so desperate to do special things with the children that the slightest threat to that, normally instigated by them, sends me into a berserker rage.

On one occasion I had phoned Leesa while away on tour and said, 'I'm really missing you and the boys – can we arrange to go to Legoland at the weekend?' She told the kids and they were buzzing and I spent the week not feeling as bad about being away because we were going to have a family day at the end of it. I really built it up for myself, thinking about all the rides we were going to go on, the food we'd eat and the fun we'd have.

I think it might have been fifteen minutes into the drive to Legoland when I shouted that if they didn't stop arguing I was going to abandon the day and go straight back home, becoming so desperate to sell my empty threat that I turned the car round and went the other way for a minute or so before rightly realizing that I was making the day shitter for myself as well.

Empty threats are something my kids are not fooled by. I remember pulling up at Gatwick Airport on the way to go on holiday and turning to them to tell them I was going to cancel it if they didn't sort themselves out. I didn't even manage to sound convincing to the end of the sentence. The kids were kind enough to not sarcastically go, 'Oh no, we are so worried', but I know that's what they were thinking.

We arrived at Legoland to find a queue into the car park. I could not fucking believe it. We'd had an awful drive and now we were inching our way towards a parking space, the mood in the car getting more toxic by the second. Once we made it to the front I was put under pressure to find a spot that wasn't five miles from the park entrance. This usually involves the kids telling me to park anywhere and Leesa saying, 'I don't understand why you didn't go there' a thousand times.

When we arrived at the queue to enter the park, I decided to pay extra to queue-jump. This is extortionate but to my mind is worth every penny. Or at least it would have been if there wasn't also a queue to buy the queue-jump tickets. I duly joined our third queue of the day before getting on a single ride. As we stood in the queue it felt like the mood of the day really hung in the balance. We were at the point where anything any of us said was annoying to the others. This came to a head when I realized from a sign by the kiosk that you could do the whole thing online. Amazing – Romesh to the rescue. I immediately sorted it on my phone and turned to Leesa to let her know that I was a hero. She then said to me, 'Why did we queue up if you could do it online?' to which I replied, 'Because I didn't know you could do it until we got here.' To which she said, 'If you were so keen on it, you'd think you would have looked it up' – I guess the point I'm trying to make is that we were beyond the looking glass in terms of being snappy with each other. Leesa finally said, 'OK, let's just start the day then.' The rest of the day was spent trying not to annoy each other until such time as I felt it safe to ask if she wouldn't mind driving back as I fancied a drink.

Desperate to create more of these special moments, we recently decided to set aside evenings when, after finishing schooling and work respectively, we would all sit down to watch a movie together, with each member of the family taking it in turn to choose the film. One night, the boys couldn't agree whose turn it was, and during the discussion about that decided to start farting on each other for fun. It ended up with me telling them that movie night was cancelled and they all had to go to their rooms, which was tough to sell with the farting thing being as funny as it was.

There is an argument for letting things like that go, but the problem is the kids then start behaving like that in public and it's humiliating. One of them called the other one a dick and I told them they shouldn't use words like that. They then asked if they could say 'penis' instead as it was the correct term. For some reason I agreed because I thought it would stop them – all it did was lead to a good month of them calling each other penises of different shapes and sizes. My wife wanted to take action, but I explained they would stop finding it funny after a while. Sadly that epiphany took fucking ages.

On occasion I have been guilty of encouraging the

behaviour. We were having a coffee at Warwick Castle and the boys and I thought it would be hilarious to have a belching competition. My poor wife. After a while of doing this in fits of giggles, we headed off to enjoy the rest of our day, with me mocking my wife for making such a big deal about it. Later that day I saw a tweet saying, 'Lunch at Warwick Castle ruined by listening to @romeshranga and his family burp throughout.'

The difficulty guaranteeing the behaviour of our children and myself has made us sometimes reluctant to book anywhere too posh. I took the family away to a really nice hotel a couple of years ago, the cost of which I would normally describe as rage-inducing, but I had decided the family deserved a treat.

I am inconsistent when it comes to the cost of things. It's pretty maddening for the children where I put my foot down. For example, because I wear stupidly priced footwear, my barometer for what is OK to spend on their clothes and shoes is skewed, but I will go absolutely bananas at them if I think they are taking the piss with pic'n'mix at the cinema. Similarly, I'm happy to pay through the nose for a nice holiday for us all, but if we have to pay too much for the crazy golf once we're there, I will moan about it to such a level that I am pretty sure the kids will forever associate crazy golf with misery and deep trauma.

The hotel was incredible – the staff treat you so well it looks a little bit arse-kissy, and everything is taken care of for you. It was so slick that I actually found it slightly embarrassing. There is something about people doing things for you that you could just as easily do yourself that

I find awkward. I try to reconcile it by imagining that if I did all that myself these people wouldn't have a job and so it is my civic duty to help employment numbers by being lazy and pathetic.

It was when we went down to the restaurant that it occurred to me we may have made a mistake. We walked into a beautiful dining area that was so quiet and civilized all you could hear was quiet conversation and the clink of cutlery against expensive plates. I looked at Leesa, and we both simultaneously realized that there was too much Crawley in us to fully enjoy having a meal there, or to have a hope in hell of our three boys not destroying the serenity of the environment. And so we turned around, headed out of the hotel and had dinner at a Pizza Express down the road. To anybody enjoying a quiet meal at that hotel – you're welcome.

Relationships

I have to confess to not knowing what romance is at this stage. When you have been together as long as we have, it's like you are just forcing yourself through the motions for the sake of not feeling like you've given up.

A few months ago, Leesa was due to have a girls' night out, and I had a gig down the road to try out new material. The girls' night fell through and she was going to cancel the babysitter when I suggested she came to the gig with me and we had a meal afterwards. I do want to take this opportunity to say that I'm not the sort of narcissist who thinks going to one of my gigs is a great night out for my wife. It was the second part of the evening that was supposed to entice her. She agreed, and we spent some time smugly discussing how great it was that we were still doing romantic things, as if going out for dinner together was something revolutionary.

The night came round and our babysitter arrived. I find babysitters terrifying, because they are always very young and I am very conscious about the fact that we are a vision of a future that is bleak and dull. I therefore try to be interesting and funny in the hope that they might not be utterly depressed by spending an evening in our home.

This is a marked change from how I initially behaved around babysitters, where I was so utterly terrified of looking predatory or pervy that I would essentially say nothing and leave all the talking to my wife. On a few occasions I have returned home from work to find that Leesa is still out and it has fallen to me to relieve the babysitter, which I always find horrifying. I'll ask some very perfunctory questions about how the boys were before trying to usher them to the door as quickly as possible without going anywhere near them. I've even been known to do this from a different room under the pretence of urgently having to check my correspondence at 9.30 p.m.

There was one particularly awkward situation where I arrived home to find the babysitter watching *Magic Mike XL*. I happen to think the first Magic Mike is a stone-cold banger, but I also think the sequel is an atrocity. I decided that rather than running away I might actually talk to the babysitter like a normal human being. I sat down and expressed my Magic Mike views and she expressed hers. Great. That felt fine. I have managed to speak to the babysitter without freaking out. Wonderful. I asked her how she was getting home – classic usher-to-the-door question. She said that she had her car with her. Brilliant.

But then, she didn't leave. She just sat there and continued to watch the film. I sat across the living room watching it, assuming she was just slightly distracted and would leave any second. But she didn't. She just sat there watching. I didn't know what the hell to do. I didn't want to watch Magic Mike but now, not only was I being forced to watch it, I was being forced to watch it with a stranger in my house. I wondered if she was too engrossed in the movie to appreciate she was behaving like a fucking lunatic, so I started saying things to try and bump her out of the movie so she would realize she wasn't at home. 'Were you able to find drinks and snacks OK? I know it can be weird when you're not at your own house.' I think I was trying to Derren Brown her into going home. She answered my questions and carried on watching the film.

I was lost at this point, as well as being furious with myself. Why couldn't I have just said hello and then gone off to check the mail? I had sat down and talked about how I liked Magic Mike and she clearly thought that meant I wanted us to watch it together. Jesus Christ. Now I was just going to have to wait it out. This was made difficult by how shit the film is, but also by the fact that the film has an incredibly long runtime. In addition, if I was choosing to watch a film with a girl I didn't know who was young enough to be my daughter, it wouldn't be one where a bunch of ripped dudes pelvically gyrate and grind up against a series of different women for two hours. To be honest, though, the whole experience was so awful that the movie choice was the least of my problems. That set-up would have even ruined *Avengers: Infinity War.*

When the film eventually finished, I prayed this wasn't part of some sort of Channing Tatum evening where she would settle down to watch the next one. Thankfully she decided that was an appropriate time to leave and she headed off, with me slamming the door behind her and hoping her interpretation of the last few hours wasn't that I had invited her to join me for a private screening of Magic Mike – that's a story I wouldn't want getting out.

This evening's babysitter in place, we headed out for the gig, at which point I became acutely nervous about Leesa coming to watch me perform. Stephen Grant is a good friend of mine and he always lets me go on at his comedy night at the Komedia in Brighton to try out new stuff. This is very kind of him, but the problem is that he always books incredible acts. I rock up with some material I've written that day, which means the audience often leave having watched me be easily the worst act on. This is fine because it's part of a learning curve and it's the process of writing new stand-up, but Leesa hadn't seen me at work for ages and I weirdly started becoming anxious about what she'd think.

I needn't have worried because she was so uninterested she didn't bother to watch me. She spent the whole time chatting to the other acts backstage. I have to confess to feeling slightly self-conscious about being at work with Leesa. The thing I'm worried about is being one of those guys who behaves differently when his wife is around. We all know them. There are varying degrees of this but, to my mind, two are the worst.

The first is the guy who changes his whole personality when his other half is within earshot. You know those people who are gregarious and chatty when on their own and suddenly brooding and quiet when their partner is around. Then during the evening they realize they've been quiet for a while, at which point they'll come out with something, when their partner will look at them incredulously before delivering an eye roll that shuts them up for the rest of the night.

Even worse than that, though, and this tends to be far more typical of men than women, is the guy whose whole schtick is to rip it out of their other half. They essentially spend the evening roasting them, every single thing they say another opportunity for a gag. Every single time their partner goes to make an observation they will say, 'That makes absolutely no sense, you mad twat!' and then look to the rest of the group and laugh. The group then laugh uncomfortably while trying to figure out a way to get the woman on her own so they can tell her to leave him immediately.

That's what I fear I am closest to behaving like. In private, Leesa and I are constantly taking the piss out of each other. It's how we survive. The problem is, when we are around other people, she feels less comfortable about doing that and is able to filter it, whereas I don't and can't. This has the effect of making me look like an absolute prick. I realize that sounds like the protest of a man who is, in actual fact, an absolute prick, but I am genuinely concerned that I give a fairly bad account of myself in these situations.

The worst is at the school gates. I cannot stand the school gates. Because I have such a low retention rate for small-talk information, the opportunities for me to drop an absolute fucking clanger are infinite. I'll forget the name of somebody I've met numerous times, I'll engage in a long chat with someone before realizing they're not who I thought they were and are in fact a stranger, I'll ask somebody how their husband is when they've told me he died the week before – have I mentioned I'm a prick? Me getting involved in the school drop-offs is basically me turning up to do a prick cameo and leaving. I used to be paranoid about it, but I have now accepted it's just going to happen. I almost embrace it. Add Leesa into this mix, though, and you have a spectacular opportunity for me to embarrass myself.

On the way to school recently I had been teasing Leesa about her going on about how busy she is. She was giving as good as she got. When we arrived at school we dropped the kids off and were just about to leave when I bumped into another mum. We did the small-talk thing and she asked me what we were up to today. For some reason I decided to carry on our running joke to a woman who'd had no previous part in the conversation. I immediately went, 'Well, I'm off to work now and she's doing absolutely fuck-all – as usual.' I don't know what reaction I was hoping for but it definitely wasn't a look of horror on the woman's face that suggested she thought Leesa was in an abusive relationship. I don't know what I was thinking. I have spoken to that woman about five times in my life. That means at least 20 per cent of the time she has interacted with me, I have been a bell-end. That's part of the problem with not remembering anybody – you don't know how well you know them and so you end up saying something that they don't know you well enough to know is a joke.

We left the Komedia and headed off to have our meal. As we left the club, one of us said, 'Can you be bothered to do dinner now?' We both agreed that it sounded like an unbearable pain in the arse, so we decided to bin off the restaurant and do something so dull I can't even believe I'm writing it. We decided to go to Tesco, buy a load of snacks and have a night in watching films. And so it came to pass. We popped into the supermarket and spent our date night selecting crisps.

It was on the way home from the supermarket that it occurred to us that we were going to have to explain to the babysitter why we had arrived home early with Tesco shopping. I imagined she would take one look at us, and immediately decide she was never going to be in a relationship ever.

It was about then that we made the most tragic decision of our evening – we went to the pub to have a drink, just to kill enough time to make us not look like losers. Shall we be honest – that is one of the most pathetic things ever, isn't it? The truth is, though, we did have a laugh – it was nice to chat, and we laughed about how sad we are, and we commented on the fact that the most excitement we were having was that they had the chilli crisps we really like. Then, having killed enough time, we rolled in at the absolutely irresponsible hour of 10.15 p.m. The babysitter must have thought we were fucking lunatics.

I had a very different idea of what love was going to look like when I was younger. My mum and dad weren't the best example of a functioning relationship – they spent most of their time arguing when we were growing up – but they did love each other. The love that is packaged and sold in films and songs is the early bit – the falling-in-love bit. I realize that's the exciting bit, and far more interesting than watching two people who have been together for ten years buy a new living-room light fitting before arguing about whose mother is the worst, but that's what most of love is. That's part of the reason I loved the film *Up* so much. It was a story of two people who spent their whole lives together.

I had spent my early life thinking I wanted to be in a relationship where we would keep that heady early bit going until we died. We would constantly be surprising each other with incredible mad nights out, we would dance the night away and then return home to pounce on each other and spend the whole night at it like wildcats. I don't know how wildcats shag, but I think you could pretty much say any animal except maybe pandas and sloths and people know that means you're really going for it.

There are couples like that. There are people who are constantly whisking each other off for mad weekends of drinking, eating and smashing, and when you talk to them they cannot stop touching each other or playing with each other's hair or kissing each other. It's impressive, and when I see them I really do think, with all of my heart: go fuck yourself. I'm deeply sceptical of anything that looks too perfect, and I can't believe those couples don't go home and have huge blowouts about the sell-by date of a yoghurt in the fridge.

Just this morning, I asked my wife if she could get some Shreddies from the local shop. What I thought I was saying was, 'Leesa, I know you are likely to be heading to the shop later on, would you mind adding Shreddies to the list?' What Leesa heard was, 'Hey, Leesa, I can't be bothered to go to the shop, so I'm ordering you to get my Shreddies like you're my personal Deliveroo. Fuck you very much!' A small argument ensued. It wasn't a huge row. I would liken it to when you see two lions eating a gazelle, and they have a little bit of a swipe at each other for getting in the way, and then carry on with their day. I guess what I'm saying is my marriage is like two wildcats picking over a carcass.

We don't often have huge rows. I wouldn't say I've ever felt smug about that, because I don't automatically think it's a good thing. I was once in a long-term relationship where we didn't argue at all, until one day we realized we were just cohabiting friends. A while ago, Leesa was telling me about a couple she knew who were having problems and couldn't stop arguing, and then we did that thing where you judge the other couple and get all smug about how much better your relationship is. It was pretty disgusting. It was then that I made the mistake of suggesting that I couldn't even imagine what we would find to argue about.

Leesa thought about this for a moment, before saying she might eventually find it a bit annoying how I sometimes don't put things in the dishwasher, or how I sometimes think I've made the bed, only for her to have to remake it, or how when I trim my beard I manage to get hair on every single surface of the building, or how sometimes when she's telling me a story I get distracted by an email. As she warmed to her theme, I essentially found myself at my own character assassination.

My problem wasn't that she got annoyed by any of those things. You yourself probably read them and thought, 'It must be really awful to live with that guy.' I am unacceptable in many ways. But that wasn't my main concern. My main concern was that she hadn't mentioned any of those things before. Which meant that she was storing all these reasons silently in her head until such time as they outweigh the positives and she leaves me alone in this hairy house. When I challenged her on this, she just laughed and said, 'But despite all that, I love you!'

She was partly joking about my bad habits, but in truth that's not reassuring at all. I was hoping she'd counter her list of criticism with some genuine reasons why I was a good husband, not a dismissive 'love you' cover-up as if she was trying to bring a phone call to an end. I certainly wasn't going to ask for them like a psychopath. I don't think there is anything quite as revolting as seeing someone asking their partner why they love them, essentially demanding a praise monologue that will never be long enough to satisfy their narcissism.

I recently sat down and watched the entirety of *Love is Blind*, a show I simultaneously enjoyed while also becoming convinced that the human race's time on the planet needs to be brought to a swift end. It is a show where people decide to partner up without seeing each other, which is a premise that seems interesting apart from the fact that all the people involved are really good-looking, and also that many of them should not have been allowed to take part for mental-health reasons.

After they have partnered up, they are then revealed to

each other. All of them talk about what they think the other one might look like, and how it doesn't matter to them because they are in love and it's all very sweet, but not one of them expresses anything about the crippling anxiety you might have about being revealed and the other person thinking you're hideous. That didn't seem to occur to them. That's all I would be thinking about.

One of the contestants or participants, or twats, who took part, early on in the process asked the guy she was paired up with to tell her why he loved her, to which my response would have been, 'Because you don't normally ask narcissistic questions like this.' This mug duly listed what he perceived to be her qualities, which, much less than being specific to her, were the usual generic things a person might like to hear about themselves: 'You are so kind, you think of others before yourself, you have such a positive energy.'

That show did make me reflect on what love is, however. This is a tricky avenue to go down and I have talked about it on stage, only for the audience to get nervous and assume that what I'm saying is I don't love my wife. But I do think the idea of loving somebody for ever is a difficult concept, and I am about to explore it here, hoping that Leesa never reads this.

Two people fall in love: they have common interests, they make each other laugh and they are sexually attracted to each other. They promise themselves to each other for ever. Then they stay together, regardless of any changes they go through that take them away from the people they originally were, the two people who fell in love with each other.

For example, I've become a vegan since Leesa and I got together. This affects the food we buy, where we go to eat, and even where we take the kids. She also has the added distress as a non-vegan of knowing that I am a better person than her. Now, obviously, if Leesa turned to me and said she was leaving me because I was vegan, I would assume she was seeing someone else and was so tired from shagging this guy that she didn't have the energy to think up a decent excuse. But the point still stands that if you have a lot of changes in your relationship, it might make you think about whether, if you knew this was the deal, you would have gone ahead with it.

I was watching *Loose Women* recently and they were talking about giving up drinking, something I have dabbled with. One of the presenters talked about how her husband had stopped drinking and it had changed their lives for the worse. Their social life had altered and she felt less comfortable about drinking in the evenings. This all really does make you ask yourself the question: 'Why the fuck am I watching *Loose Women*?'

This is all academic, of course, because I feel like I love my wife more than I ever have, and I think she very much loves me, but my point is that it is not an objective decision. We are bound to each other by the intense conditioning programme that is getting-married-and-having-children.

I do worry about how I'm doing as a husband. There are the obvious things to think about, like remembering birthdays and anniversaries, and making some sort of effort to keep the romance going. I have to confess to being fairly shit at this side of things. I get caught up in the day-to-day, and forward planning doesn't come easily. Some years I manage to pull something together and give Leesa a nice day and a series of presents. The next year I might just get her a card. I suspect this is the worst possible situation for her. She has to feign gratitude regardless of what is delivered. Obviously she needs to do that when the kids give her the pasta jewellery they've made at school, but you shouldn't have to do that with your husband. That poor woman has to spend the nights before her birthday not sure whether she is going to get a holiday, or a piece of A4 paper folded in two with 'World's Best Wife and Mum' written on it in crayon. It's psychological torture.

This bleeds into everyday life too. I'm so poorly organized that most of my life is spent dealing with being behind with something or late for something. This means I am often rushing around the house with less than due diligence, blissfully ignoring the aftermath that my panic tornado is leaving in its wake.

For example, I might be on my way to work, and in a hurry to eat something before I leave to catch the train that is already two trains after the one that would have got me to the meeting on time. I drop some Shreddies on the floor. To my mind, those Shreddies are not an immediate threat. They are not a biohazard, nor are they likely to explode, and so I might roughly tidy them up and put them in the bin, with some crumbs and fragments remaining for me to tidy up when I return. The message I think I am sending Leesa is, 'Hey, babe! I was in a bit of a rush for work, which I do to make our lives better, and I dropped some Shreddies! Really sorry, didn't have time to properly get all the crumbs but will do it when I get back! Love you so much!' The message I am actually sending is, 'Hey, Leesa, you prick! You know those Shreddies I asked you to get? Well, I spilled them on the floor and didn't tidy them up properly and now you're going to clean it up and I'll forget when I get back and not even thank you!'

These alternative views of events are not generally something Leesa shares with me, bar the night she performed her roast of me, but this is something I have made an effort to be more aware of. I read a transcript of a commencement speech by the late author David Foster Wallace, in which he said we are all hardwired to believe we are the centre of the universe – everything happens to us, the world is doing things to us. His point was that as soon as you start to try and overcome that hardwiring and think of things from other people's perspectives, life becomes a lot easier.

My accidental lack of consideration meets with Leesa's silent tolerance and I have had to become more mindful of that. Helping out more isn't always thc solution, however, because Leesa and I do not seem to have the same pass mark when it comes to a job being done or not. The other night I came home from work just as Leesa was getting the boys ready for bed. I decided to clean up all their dinner stuff and sort out the kitchen. I cleaned the kitchen top to bottom, and then went upstairs to claim my thank-you sex.

The message I was sending Leesa on that occasion was, 'Hey, Leesa, you shithead! I have cleaned the kitchen to such a substandard level that you are going to have to do it all over again and then I am going to expect you to be grateful to me for saving you absolutely no time at all! Go fuck yourself!'

For all of my pontifications, however, I genuinely believe that I am currently in the best part of my relationship – knowing each other fully, completely being ourselves and loving each other for that. It's not as exciting or as sexy as that getting-to-know-you bit at the beginning, but it's great. I intend to enjoy it to its fullest before we move on to the bit where we start deeply resenting each other and I bring out my book on divorce.

Getting Old

I used to think I didn't give a shit about getting older. Then one day I saw how many grey hairs I had in my hair and beard and I felt disgusted. I don't think it was because of my actual age – I certainly don't have any sort of crisis every time my birthday comes around – but I think the physical signs of ageing make me look rank. It looks like there are these grey spiders trying to escape from my face. Leesa keeps telling me it's a salt-and-pepper look, but salt-and-pepper is nicely and evenly distributed grey, not clumps of it like a lawn with weed-killer spilt on it.

At first I resisted dyeing it, mainly because of my uncles, a group of men in their seventies who all have jet black hair, which looks insane. For a while, I decided that plucking was the sensible option. It achieved the effect without me having to put rubber gloves on and admit that I had lost my battle with vanity. I started to find plucking annoying – I am vain enough to want to pluck my grey hair, but too lazy to actually bother doing it, so I needed another solution. After a while it became clear that dyeing would be the easier option, but I held off because that felt like me admitting I cared about getting older. And it throws up other questions – the biggest of which is, when do you stop? I'm forty-two now, so it's reasonable for me to have black hair, but there will be a point at which it will become obvious that I'm dyeing it. Dyeing your greys is a hard thing to reverse out of, and I don't want that point to arrive. So what do you do? As far as I can tell your only real strategy is to plan your storyline long-term like *Breaking Bad*. You decide when your going-grey period is going to be and you work towards that deadline. As that time arrives, you control the grey coming in, so that people don't think it's weird that you suddenly started greying out at 85 years old. I feel like I may have thought about this too much.

The moment arrived when I finally caved in. A friend of mine recommended a shampoo-in colour product. He said it would take five minutes and looked really natural. This seemed like a bit of a no-brainer and so I bought some. Leesa has been very much against me getting rid of my greys. She keeps telling me it's sophisticated, but that to me does not equate to being attractive. Nobody has ever said, 'God, that guy is really turning me on with how distinguished he looks. I bet he knows his way around a Poirot box set.'

With Leesa's protestations ringing in my ears I decided I would wait until I was away to use my youth elixir. I was in Manchester on tour and had a plan. I was going to check in, apply the dye, come downstairs looking ten years younger, and use that new-found confidence to absolutely smash the gig that evening. I applied the dye and waited the appropriate time. The brain plays a weird mental trick when you are waiting for something like this. A few minutes feels like the widest ocean of time imaginable. I had to leave it in for five minutes. Five minutes just passed between me writing this sentence and the last one. It's nothing. Make it an amount of time to wait before you can wash out hair dye and it feels like a lifetime. I started thinking about how I was going to survive the wait. Maybe I could make some phone calls to friends I haven't spoken to in a while – perhaps I should start writing that children's book?

I got into the shower after the eternity and rinsed the dye out of my hair, excited to see how I looked. I was so keen I kept trying to angle a mirror glance from the shower, but then realized that no amount of hair youth could counter-balance the sight of my flabby body so I decided against. When I did emerge from the shower, who was this young Romesh I saw in the mirror before me? OK, I exaggerate, but I was pretty happy with how it had sort of worked without me looking like I'd taken shoe polish to my head.

I was just about to FaceTime Leesa to get her all hot and bothered with my sexy new look when I noticed there was some dye still in the bathtub. 'Let me just rinse that out before my phone sex with Leesa,' I thought as I turned the shower on. The dye didn't move. 'Maybe it needs a bit of a rub,' I thought. That didn't work either. 'Maybe it needs some soap,' I thought, my internal monologue taking on a slight tone of concern. It was about a minute into using the soap that my brain went, 'Maybe you've dyed the bathtub, you absolute fucking idiot.'

That is certainly what it looked like I'd done. Fucking hell. This was a nightmare. All of the worst-case scenarios started flooding my brain: the hotel guys recognized me, they're going to tell people I stained the tub – worse, they might think it's the remnants of some sort of weird orgy where I shagged a hooker in the bath with indelible ink or something. I mean, I was panicking.

This wasn't even the first time I'd caused damage in the hotel. Just the previous year I had been staying there during my book tour and spilled some beard oil (I know) on a futon in the room. I immediately threw some water on it to scrub it off. Then I was worried that I hadn't cleaned it properly because there was a wet patch. I therefore had the bright idea of using a hairdryer to dry it so I could see. I put the hairdryer on to the seat and about ten seconds in I began to smell burning. I picked the hairdryer up to find I had burned a perfect circle into the futon.

There was definitely going to be some story in the paper about me being a vandalism fetishist or something. I panicked some more. I contemplated calling my tour manager, but then I envisioned how that was going to go down: 'Hey, mate, can you come and help me? I've managed to stain the bath tub. Little word of warning for when you get here – I look fucking amazing.'

The next two hours were spent scrubbing the shit out of that bathtub. I would scrub and check, scrub and check, over and over again until I wasn't sure if I was still seeing the stain or if it was burned into my retinas. I don't know if the fumes from the cleaning stuff were getting to me, but for a moment I considered googling bathroom shops in the area. In the end it got to the point where my hands were so sore that I decided they could just bill me for a new tub. Until I caught a glimpse of myself in the mirror and realized it had all been worth it.

Having sorted out my greys, I really don't know how I feel about ageing now. I find myself talking to people in their twenties and thinking we are having a conversation as friends, until I remember back to my twenties and remember how ancient I thought people in their forties were. It doesn't feel old to me now, and in many ways I still feel like I'm not ready to do any grown-up things, but that might be more down to general disfunction than a young spirit.

And there is something wonderful about getting older. You become more comfortable in your own saggy skin. You don't give as much of a shit about people's perceptions of you, and so you find yourself more inclined to do what you want to do. I do find myself wondering about the effect of age on my work, however. I don't think it's a coincidence that many artists' best work is when they first emerge: it's raw and it's them, undiluted by expectation or previous success or even the pressure of life not matching up to how you imagined it.

Stand-up rewards experience to a degree, but your senses become dulled by comfort, reputation, and a fear of undermining the success or popularity you have acquired so far. It's part of the reason I love Richard Pryor so much – he was on the way to the top as a mainstream comic, then one day decided to throw it all away and disappeared. When he came back, he was the all-time great we know and remember now. Dave Chappelle, somebody I also admire hugely, did something very similar. Before I get too comfortable and safe I might have to disappear for a bit too. My only fear is that I will come back having got no better, nobody will offer me any work and you'll see me exit round 1 on *The Masked Singer.*

I had always assumed I would be very chilled out about looking and getting older, especially when I haven't exactly been smashing it in my prime. And yet I find myself comparing photos of me now with ones from the past and feeling the sting of knowing that you can see the years on me. I think it's the fear of irrelevance that is the worst. Older people's views in this country hold less weight than they used to. Younger people don't give a shiny shit what older people have to say any more. And so you feel like you're getting closer to becoming the part of society that people listen to because they feel they are supposed to rather than because they want to or have any respect for the wisdom of your years. Conversations increasingly become a series of clipped standard questions like, 'How have you been bearing up? What have you been eating?' and 'Is that smell you?'

I'm part of the culture that I fear will ignore me later in life. I really need to be showing more respect to our elderly. And by respect, I mean both listening to and engaging with them properly like humans, but also not being amazed and patronizing when they are able to do anything at all, like you've just seen a dog solve a Rubik's cube. If we treated our elderly better and listened to them more, there would be a myriad of advantages. First, on a human level it's nicer to be nice to people, especially if they've been through a lot, as anyone who's lived for eighty years is bound to have been. Secondly, we might be able to gain some advantages from tapping into this whole sector of society who have already seen and done it all. I realize that the idea of talking to elderly people can seem intimidating and weird to younger generations, but old people are made intimidating and weird by their lack of interaction with people. Have you ever had a couple of days where you sit at home doing nothing and then the first time you go out and talk to someone, you're so unused to it that you do a brain fart and say something like, 'Trifle is good'? Try having no interaction for weeks at a time and see how sharp your chat is then. I am convinced there are reserves of old people chat that we are not tapping. They just need warming up a bit with some starter conversation.

The biggest advantage of treating old people better and incorporating them more into society is that people won't be so frightened of becoming old and 'irrelevant' themselves. They'll realize it is a natural progression and it's not worse than, just different to, youth, and then we won't see more and more people turning themselves into lizard-lookalikes because they are so scared of looking over forty.

I am now on a mission to embrace age. I've already started preparing my stand-up tour where all the observations will be about how my bladder has lost its elasticity and how it's really awkward when you fancy one of your carers. And for the finale I'm going to do something like half-arsedly carry a tune and do a little dance, because when young people see the elderly doing that on *Britain's Got Talent* they lose their shit.

Discretion

I wrote most of my Cynic's Mixtape tour in Crawley, which sounds like an incredibly obvious thing to say given that I live there, but what I mean is that I would work up half an hour to an hour of material, book the small studio room at the Hawth theatre in town and try the stuff out there. I put my trust in the people of Crawley to guide me as to the quality of the set I was piecing together. It's a weird experience doing so many gigs so close to where you live. As I was going through that writing process I would be at the pub with my family for lunch and someone would come up to me and say, 'Definitely keep in the bit about Batman' or, more often than not, 'I can't believe you told that story about your mum.' Then my mum would ask me what they meant and lunch would be ruined.

Crawley audiences have seen the absolute worst of me. When you write new material, you can sometimes go too far for the laugh. My routines often start way too offensive or revealing and the audience response usually helps me dial them back to something more acceptable. One day I'm going to do a tour of the totally unfiltered, vilest stories I've thought of and see if anyone comes to that – that will probably be my retirement tour, after which I may as well burn my house down and leave the country.

One of the sections of the Cynic's Mixtape tour details my decaying sex life with my wife. I think decaying might be a bit strong, but it's definitely not fresh. This was another routine I worked out at the Hawth, which, thinking about it, is a pretty horrendous thing to do to my wife. I can't imagine what it must have been like to do the school drop-off the following week and have one of her friends approach her and say, 'I hear you aren't putting out very much at the moment.'

A couple we know had asked us to go to dinner on the night I had a warm-up show, and so they suggested coming to the gig and doing dinner afterwards. As I was getting ready to go onstage, Leesa popped into the dressing room to wish me luck. As she went to leave I remembered what I was going to be trying out and I said, 'Oh, there's this bit about our sex life I'm going to be doing tonight.' Leesa really doesn't mind what I talk about on stage, and so she wished me luck and said if I talked about having a big dick she would call me out. Leesa is to blame for a lot of the offence I have caused. People often ask me if she minds me talking about her and she genuinely just sees it all as jokes and comedy and therefore meaningless. Which means I get all blasé about it and think it's fine and then all of her friends think I'm a bastard.

Obviously, I hadn't honed the routine at this point, I was literally just saying the words for the first time to see if there was anything funny in it, and so it was a pretty frank discussion of what Leesa and I were experiencing passion-wise. I have a vivid memory of seeing Leesa's face in the audience looking completely calm, and then glancing across to our friends next to her, who looked utterly horrified at the prospect of going out for dinner with a couple they now knew were definitely not having sex when they got home afterwards. As we all rather quietly made our way to the restaurant it occurred to me that I should think a bit more carefully about how I aired our family laundry on stage. Then the food arrived and I forgot all about it.

It's not just saying too much onstage that I worry about. I've become conscious about how much shit talking goes on in everyday conversations. One of the things I've always observed is how negative people are behind other people's backs. There are WhatsApp groups I am a part of that solely exist to identify something embarrassing or shit or awful that people we know have done. They are then unknowingly subjected to an absolute pasting by a group of guys on a private chat. It's like the WI on steroids, emboldened by smartphones. It feels like a great laugh and is born from insecurity, but I have become convinced it's not good for the soul. Don't get me wrong, I have not become unfalteringly positive about everything I see people doing, but I am trying to make a concerted effort to not be the person who picks them apart.

Gossip seems to be our favourite pastime, and according to some neuroscientists it has played a critical role in our development as a species. But it's amazing how much is said about us that we never find out about – unless somebody slips up and accidentally texts their criticism to us. I have been guilty of this, sending a text about someone to that very person by mistake. I tried to cover it up, which is even worse. Far more honourable to send a follow-up message that says, 'So that last text, if you're wondering, is just confirmation that I'm an arsehole.'

I tried discussing all of this onstage, but the general public do not feel comfortable about laughing at things like that. When you laugh at something, you are communicating that you agree with it and relate to it. People don't always feel able to publicly laugh at something shameful or uncomfortable because it confirms they are doing it too. To use an extreme example, it would be like hearing a comedian going, 'Aren't coloured people awful?!' You would immediately judge anyone who laughed. People don't want to be outed as gossips. Or racists. Or racist gossips.

The need to discuss and critique others definitely comes from insecurity, though. You want to share with somebody what you think of somebody else and you want them to agree with you. You want validation. And picking holes in someone else's life makes you both feel better about your own. It's like when you and your partner go to see somebody's new house, and you're being shown around and it's all lovely. The hosts give you the tour and you ooh and aah and comment on how lucky they are and 'Doesn't it make our place look tatty?' etc. (I don't know why suddenly I think I would use the word 'tatty' but it's you in this analogy not me.) You have dinner in their lovely new dining area and then head off home. You both talk politely and calmly about how nice the place was. Then you go quiet. Then one of you goes, 'I didn't like how they did

75

the bathroom.' And you go, 'I know!!' and then you spend the next hour discussing everything you hated about the house.

That's obviously not really you hating the house. That's you being insecure about them having a nice house and comforting each other by pretending the house is awful. That's what we're doing when we slag people off. It's all a desperate attempt by us to forget how utterly shit we think we are. It's a rank side of human nature. The people who don't have that in them, and seem to be truly happy for other people's success, tend to be happier people generally. Don't get me wrong – they are also fucking insufferable, but they don't care.

So, be discreet, and try not to be a dick. And if you are a dick, at least try to be discreet about it.

Other People's Children

One of the things that genuinely concerns me is other people's perception of how I interact with my children. I don't mean, 'Are the Ranganathan boys being pushed hard enough academically?' I just mean general day-to-day interactions with my children and how people see me as a parent.

This is very unlike me. I normally don't give a shiny shit about what people think of how I do things, but there is something terrifying about thinking you might have spoken or acted in a way that suggests you could be an abusive parent, or negligent or something. I've lost count of the number of times I've seen somebody screaming at their kid and thought, 'Bloody hell, that seems a bit full-on.' Now, I'm absolutely not judging the parent here – being a parent is stressful and you get tired and you react in ways you're not proud of – but at the same time the kid doesn't know that and it's pretty shitty. You'll be in the middle of some work thing that is going particularly badly and your kid will ask if you can fix their Lego model, and then you go, 'Does that absolutely have to happen now?! I'm working!', and the kid feels awful despite the fact at no point did they suggest it absolutely had to be done immediately.

Similarly, I am infuriated with parents who don't keep their kids in line, particularly when they are at someone else's house. If my kids step out of line at a friend's house I'm so embarrassed that I go way over the top. I've been known to issue a month-long gaming ban for a crisp being dropped on the floor. This, of course, then leads to crying at the injustice of the punishment, and I have to pretend that I don't completely agree with them, and Leesa looks at me incredulously as we either have to endure the worst month of our lives trying to enforce the ridiculous ban or undermine the whole threat of punishment for ever.

I remember one time during the Christmas/New Year gooch, a couple of friends came over with their daughter. We still had some presents under the tree because the boys were of the ages where they received a thousand presents each from friends and family, and we thought we would stagger out the opening in a bid to make sure they fully appreciated everything they were getting. While we were chatting, the girl started demanding that one of the presents was opened so she could see what it was. I would describe this request as clearly unacceptable, although I acknowledge that the fact our children receive more presents than they can open in a day is privilege in a nutshell. But what you call privilege I call Asian grandparents. I waited quietly for this to be shut down. It wasn't. In fact, it was handled in a way that suggested the parents actually wanted us to open a present to bring this situation to a close for them. And that is what we did, one of our sons opening a present and showing her what it was, whereupon she realized, as we had all warned, that it was of no interest because our kids were much younger than her.

We carried on our conversation only to have this girl then enquire about another one of the presents. We waited for this to be shut down, but of course her demands led to another present being opened. This continued until our boys had opened every single one of their Christmas presents, at which point they went upstairs to sulk about having to open them all for this visitor they didn't even know.

Eventually it was time for them to go, which I had been waiting for earnestly because I really was busting to have that post-visit 'what the fuck was that about' debrief, when they said that on the way home they were going to get ice cream to reward their daughter for being so good.

It was as much as I could do not to get up and shout, 'Oh really? Well, why bother going to the shop? I am sure we have some ice cream for our children that you can just take with you, you absolute fuckwits.' Obviously I didn't do that. I just remarked on how well behaved she had been and offered them some ice cream. Thankfully they declined and left. We were so furious and judgy about what had just happened that I actually enjoyed the rage. Plus, when you are as prone to errors of judgement as I am, it feels pretty cathartic to be able to throw some shit at other people for a change.

Leesa had made friends with a couple whose children go to the same school as ours. As I've said, while I'm pretty much closed to new friendship applications, Leesa is still making a valiant effort to add to our social circle. The trouble is, because I'm so shit at small talk and engaging with people, every time we go out it's a roll of the dice as to whether the people we meet will want to do it again.

We'd been invited over to their house, and during the course of the evening I got wound up by the fact that Leesa was making jokes about how I, because I'm away from home working so much, really don't have a clue how to look after the kids. This couple were laughing and we were all having a wonderful time talking about what a useless prick I am. In a bid to defend my name, every time our kids came into the room I would start overcompensating and being really 'Dad-ish' with them, as if to prove that I did know how to interact with my children. This had the effect of making me look like a parental David Brent, and our kids stared at me like I was some sort of lunatic.

At one point, the kids started having a Nerf fight, and every time they ran through where we were sitting I would yet again say something wankery like, 'It's good to see you having fun, kids, but remember to play safe.' The kids by this point had accepted that I had decided to play the part of responsible father for the evening. Job done. I was going to end the night with these people mistakenly thinking I am, in fact, an effective parent.

It was as we were going to leave that things fell apart. We were putting our coats on and the kids were still running around playing with the guns. I decided I wanted to put some icing on this cake and give the impression that I was also a fun dad. I grabbed one of the guns and started shooting at all the children. What a master plan, Romesh! These people are going to think you're absolutely marvellous. I'm sure that after you leave they will talk about what a brilliant father you are, and how lucky Leesa is to have you!

It was around the time that I was having this internal

celebration monologue that I shot our eldest son straight in the eye. I don't mean near the eye, I don't mean the eyelid, I mean directly into the eyeball. I mean, it looked like I was deliberately trying to blind him. He started screaming, and everyone turned to look at me as if trying to understand what the hell I was playing at. All I had had to do was to leave quietly, but for some reason I had decided to ruin the whole evening by physically wounding my son. I asked my son if he was OK, to which he replied no, in an attempt I think to encourage these people to call social services. What should have been goodbyes were instead apologies as my son received rudimentary medical treatment and I tried to pretend I was feeling extremely casual about what had just gone down.

We left, and I imagine that couple discussed how awful I was as a father. I could only dream of being the parents whose kids asked to open someone else's presents. The biggest fear I had is that they would assume I was trying to give my son an eye like mine in some sort of family tradition. 'Oh, you know, in Sri Lankan culture, instead of a bar mitzvah they get the kid on his thirteenth birthday to take a point blank Nerf to the retina. It's tradition. It's why Sri Lankans have absolutely no depth perception.'

If you're a parent, you always think you're getting it wrong, but be reassured by the fact everybody else is too.

Video Games

There was a time when I was absolutely banging at video games. I used to buy consoles as soon as they came out and I would play them to death, never losing patience, completing games left, right and centre and being surprised that it didn't impress girls. My dad used to occasionally join in with my brother and me, and he was breathtakingly shit. He would find the controls utterly impenetrable and we would quickly realize that the annoyance of trying to teach him how to play cancelled out the quality time we were having with him and we would all give up. I remember thinking I was so lucky because when I went on to have kids I would be in a better position and they would find it amazing to have a father who was awesome at gaming and could beat them at everything.

That thought ran through my head again recently as I sat and watched my son knock a sixth goal past me in Rocket League, this weird 'football with cars' game the kids are obsessed with at the moment. They asked me if I wanted to join in and I said yes, anticipating a short time of getting acquainted with the controls before handing their arses to them, and teaching them a valuable lesson about competition. I couldn't even get near the fucking ball. Most of the games involved them passing between one another and scoring while I drove around the 'pitch' aimlessly like a drunk divorcé. At this point, I was unbothered. I assumed it was because the controls were not what I was used to and resolved to practise on my own after they had gone to bed, as I have done in the past when they were younger, and did on Mario Kart as a lesson to Leesa for showing me disrespect on the Wii.

Despite practising for hours, I could not discern any noticeable improvement in what I was doing. I started thinking I was making a breakthrough before realizing that I had just got lucky and was still very much, as my kids would say, 'noob trash'. This level of humiliation was only in playing against the AI teams, though. The few shreds of dignity I had left after that were set fire to when I went online. Admittedly it's a weird progression to think: 'Well, I'm complete dog shit at this easier version of the game, now let me see how that holds up against the very best people playing it across the world.' I think I had convinced myself that there was something about the computer predictability that meant I couldn't beat it but I would somehow have a better chance against actual people.

I was so appalling that I am surprised I didn't get our family banned from the internet. I imagine the people I was playing with assumed that an animal had got hold of the controller somehow, such was the complete randomness of what I was doing. I switched off the game and descended into a depression. I started googling 'effects of age on computer game reflexes'. I became convinced that

I might have dementia, and found countless videos with titles like, 'Is your brain too old for video games?'

That thought was particularly depressing, because in a world where we are constantly dealing with pulls on our attention, I have become increasingly convinced by the meditative effects of video games. It is one of the few things that somebody with an attention span like mine can remain engaged with. When I'm watching even the best TV show, I occasionally flit to my phone. I hope this book reads with the coherence of someone who has written it uninterruptedly, but the truth is that I am constantly having to remind myself to keep writing the book and not just stare into the garden. When I play video games, though, I am completely involved and think about nothing else other than trying to succeed in whatever is going on. I enjoy the fact I can switch off from everything else for a while.

What I have realized, however – and this has only come up recently – is that I only find games immersive if I'm doing well at them. Now, when I am playing with the boys and they are destroying me with no sign of even a lucky victory coming my way, then I just button-smash while thinking about ordering a takeaway.

More recently the kids have become obsessed with Fortnite, the online game where you drop on to an island and try to kill everybody else on it. I have no idea how we have got to a place where we think it's OK for our kids to be playing this, but that is where we find ourselves. The game is addictive and is all the boys talk about. You can buy skins for your character and play in teams and they have started picking up all the lingo that goes with it. The other day my son came into the bedroom and without even a 'Good morning' said, 'Dad, do you want to come and watch me get sweaty with a default?' Even besides the fact that it sounds like a niche Pornhub search, I have to say I find this new slang insane. Of course, my kids accuse me of being an out-of-touch old man.

The low point came when one morning they asked if I wanted to play with them. I said I was busy and they started begging. I eventually relented and they started cheering and whooping about how excited they were. I have to confess to getting a little emotional. As I walked down the stairs to join them, I saw them setting up and, not realizing I was there, talking about how funny it was going to be to play with somebody as crap as me.

I feel like an old man in particular when I see the popularity of games like Call of Duty and other high-level war simulators, where the game play is so realistic it's possible to emerge from the living room with PTSD. I actually find them worse than Fortnite because there's no blood in Fortnite and you don't really die, you kind of get beamed out of the game. Call of Duty, on the other hand, is military-grade. It's mad. I used to play war games myself as a kid, but the graphics were so shit it was barely possible to distinguish people from the pixellated background, let alone see those people die in front of you. If you shot anyone they'd just sort of comically topple over before flashing a few times and disappearing. As the years went on, the graphics got better and better until basically they are now combat training.

The difference between what I enjoyed playing as a kid then and the games my boys play now at the same age has presented an interesting dilemma, because at the risk of sounding like a hypocrite, I really don't know if kids in primary school should be playing something that has been designed to make you feel like you are in an actual warzone. However, Leesa and I have not fully figured out what our rules on this are.

To compensate for my apparent lack of gaming ability, I've started trying to find other common ground with my kids. My eldest son loves family sitcoms, and is currently ploughing his way through *The Big Bang Theory*. Comedy purists will tell me I should not allow him to pollute his mind in this way and I should get him on to Monty Python or something but I'm just delighted he has an interest in comedy, and he's ten, so fuck off. I don't want him to become a performer, but I still watch comedy more than anything else, and if he does too it will be a great thing to have in common. I'm already looking forward to introducing him to my own comedy heroes – acts like Bill Burr and Frank Skinner.

One of the other things he wanted to watch in its entirety was *Friends*, which brought my wife and I back to the conversation about what we deemed appropriate for our children. My wife became concerned about it, not in the millennial way of finding it desperately lacking in diversity and also transphobic, but because it had some sexual storylines and jokes she didn't think appropriate for someone of his age. I had to pick her up on this and ask what was the line we were drawing, because although there were indeed some sexual storylines in *Friends*, and not enough black people, it didn't seem to bother her that our son had killed thirty people that morning with impressively accurate headshots. I pointed out that it's possible that the age-inappropriate activities in *Friends* would be things he would go on to experience – sex and a lack of diversity – whereas I am hopeful that the future won't find him alone with his only means of survival being to kill everyone else on the island. We decided as a result that *Friends* is OK. I would say, however, that although when you think of *Big Bang Theory* and *Friends* they seem squeaky clean, watching them alongside one of your children illuminates how much sexual content there is in them. I felt like we were watching Pornhub together.

All this makes me think about the rules my parents set when we were growing up, which were essentially non-existent. I don't think my parents fully grasped age ratings and child suitability, which is why I was allowed to watch 18-rated films and listen to sweary hip-hop from the age of about ten. I don't know if it had a negative effect but I do swear a fuckload. My levels of hypocrisy are impressive, particularly when it comes to how kids want to spend their time. I played video games incessantly as a child, yet I find it maddening that my kids are on their consoles as much as they are. But there is no science to it. We just think that because they're playing on them so much, it's probably bad. But at least they're practising motor skills and talking to each other. We have, on more than one occasion, demanded that the kids come off the games and sit with us for a family movie night, so they can be even less active and also eat popcorn and chocolate, while resenting us because they would rather be playing Fortnite. As parenting logic goes, it's pretty twisted.

I'm sure a lot of this stems from an inherent fear we have of our kids doing anything they enjoy. We convince ourselves that things that are good for them are things they hate, so if they enjoy something too much it must be bad for them and we start figuring out how to stop it. Just this morning our son wanted yoghurt and was begging for it and so we explained he could have it as long as he had another bagel, a foodstuff I am pretty sure has absolutely no nutritional value at all. He ate the bagel to get the yoghurt, which is about as mad as forcing a child to sit through a movie before they're allowed to play video games.

I also think a big component of the whole parents vs video games debate is that parents don't like feeling left out of their children's lives. There's this whole virtual world that adults don't participate in, which scares them and – in my case – makes them feel old. That's why I became pissed off about my total lack of ability when gaming with my kids. I was desperate to find a solution partly because I like video games, but mainly because I don't like being destroyed at them by children. I googled what to do and I found that there's a whole community of retro gamers, who have ignored the new technologies and exclusively play the old games I grew up playing. I became incredibly excited and decided this was the way forward. I bought a Sega Genesis emulator so I could show the boys how good I am at all the old-school games, so they would turn to me and say, 'I can't believe we doubted you, Dad. We understand now that you are a true master and actually these new games are beneath you. We're so sorry we didn't realize what a fucking legend you are.' And then I would say something about them not using that kind of language but that I really appreciated the sentiment.

I set up the emulator and gathered the boys round to watch and join in so that they could get to figuring out how they were going to worship me as quickly as possible. We set up Sonic the Hedgehog. The boys let me have the first go. We very quickly discovered two things: 1) the game and its graphics were too basic for the boys to have any interest in, and 2) it turns out I am actually shit at the old games as well.

Culture

Doing travel shows has imbued me with such an appreciation for other cultures that I wish travel were more accessible than it is, and it is certainly something I will encourage our children to do. When we started to put together the ideas for *The Misadventures of Romesh Ranganathan*, the original plan for the show was that I would travel to the most dangerous places in the world and see if they were fun. Rumpus, the production company I had made *Asian Provocateur* with, had come up with the concept and I thought it was a good one. I had, however, forgotten that I would be the one doing the show. So when they said, 'You'll be going to dangerous places', my first instinct was, 'That will make a great show', without fully appreciating that it would be me who actually had to visit these locations. It was only when we started plotting the episodes that I started to shit myself a bit.

The premise of the show changed when a lot of the places that had been chosen were deemed too dangerous to visit and it became clear that you couldn't make a show called 'The Most Dangerous Places In The World That Aren't Too Dangerous To Film In', and so the emphasis was changed from life-threatening to unlikely travel destinations.

I'm not a hardened traveller, so even without the risk of death some of the filming was a challenge. I know, I know. 'Try working down a coal mine, Romesh.' I do not have a tough job by any stretch, but there have been some difficult moments. By the time we got to the second series, I was in a better position to handle them, and I was better prepared for the rigours of making a travel show. But I still had blind spots.

One of the things I found the most challenging on that series was our visit to Bosnia Herzegovina. I knew it was difficult to walk the line of how to cover the country's troubled past without causing offence or seeming totally ignorant. I have never managed to develop any interest in history and that hole in my knowledge has been a huge embarrassment to me. I don't know anything. I become terrified whenever history is discussed because I know I am one comment away from a hyper-thick faux pas, saying something like, 'Did Henry VIII get on with Hitler?' I know I should do something about it because I do actually believe in the value of learning from history, but so far it's just something I've worked hard to conceal, usually by deploying the classic nod-and-agree response before steering the discussion away.

I was doing a podcast with the American comedian Tom Rhodes, and we were having a relaxed conversation about nothing when he revealed that he was an avid history fan, and was particularly in love with Britain because of its close ties to its history. I nodded and agreed, without any real idea of what the fuck he was talking about, when he then asked me if there was anything in history I found particularly inspirational. I pondered this for a moment, panicking as I tried to think of an example that I wouldn't be asked to elaborate on sufficiently to the point where I was unmasked as a moron. I decided it would be much easier to be honest and say no. He then, I think disbelievingly, asked me if I was saying there was no period of history I found inspiring or interesting. I didn't have the heart to explain that I had such little inclination to research history that I couldn't even quote a period of it if I wanted to. He was pretty astounded, and I remember spending the rest of the podcast pretending to have a calm and relaxed chat with him but in actuality reeling from the embarrassment of what had happened.

I decided to remedy the situation and bought Andrew Marr's *A History of Modern Britain* as well as a book called *Prisoners of Geography* that I was assured was a dummies' guide to the history of the world. I wasn't looking to know everything, just not to make a dick of myself again. I have attempted to read both books about ten times each and can't get any further than the initial chapters. This is no slur on either book. It might just be time for me to accept that I'm ignorant. It's not that I don't have time to read. I bought *The Beastie Boys* autobiography, a terrifyingly huge tome, and read that in pretty much one sitting. I suppose that's history too, but I don't think Tom would have been that impressed if I'd told him my most inspirational period in history was the run-up to the release of the album *Hello Nasty*.

All of this is to set out the context within which I was visiting Bosnia. I suspected that the show was going to centre around Sarajevo and the conflict, and I also knew that in all likelihood, my complete lack of knowledge and understanding was going to be rightly exposed and ridiculed. The truth is, it was an absolute eye-opener. Skender, our tour guide, was exceptional company, and only too delighted to spend time explaining the history of the conflict and how it had affected the country. I became completely fascinated by the fact that such a savage war had taken place so close to us so very recently, and we had mostly ignored what was going on. One hundred thousand people died in that war in the early 1990s and it is barely spoken about today.

One of the nights in Sarajevo was to be spent at a war hotel. This hotel was run by quite a scary young man called Zero One. The idea of the hotel was that you would essentially simulate the experience of living in Sarajevo during the conflict. The commitment to this was impressive. Noises of conflict were pumped into the building at all times, and there was no running water. You would go outside to fill large bottles of water to wash and brush your teeth, and you would sleep on the floor. The lighting was minimal and you prepared your own dinner on a gas bottle provided by Zero One as he talked you through frying up some flour rings he called 'war doughnuts'. That was part of the whole experience actually. He would just prefix things with the word 'war'. He suggested I choose my war bed before getting some war water from outside so I could war brush my teeth.

I sound pretty disrespectful here, and I do not mean to, because it was clear that Zero One had been affected by his family living through the war. Rather than an insight into what it must have been like, the experience was actually a bit more of a fetishization of the war experience, with Zero One laying it on pretty thick. The highlight of this was when he offered to show me the pièce de résistance of the hotel, a war museum he had put together downstairs. This was a room full of guns and ammunition that he had collected over the years. He had then scratched various messages into the wall with a blade. I asked him if the messages were from a book or taken from things that had actually been said and he explained that they were just things he imagined people might say during the war. The walls were covered with things like 'When will this end?' and 'I hope I get some food soon. All I have is a bit of bread' – just really mad, random stuff. I could not wait to get out of there.

The maddest thing about that experience is that people absolutely love it. When you look up the comments on the hotel, visitors are effusive about the first-hand immersive experience they had, so I think we can surmise that the problem is with me rather than him. I think I probably resist whenever I feel like I'm being manipulated. I was much more moved by our visit to the Tunnel of Hope, the underground tunnel that between 1993 and 1996, while Sarajevo was under siege, was the only connection its people had with the outside world. The stories behind building and using that lifeline were something I found unexpectedly moving.

It is my resistance to feeling like I'm being pushed for an emotional response that makes me cynical about things other people tend to love. I remember being at an awards discussion and talking about how much *Britain's Got Talent*

winds me up when they play Adele and cut to Simon wink-
ing his approval to make everyone cry at the joy of somebody
being able to leave their job at Tesco. I was then essentially
set upon by everyone in the room for being heartless. I just
don't like things that feel over-produced. But I am a hypocrite, because I love all the Pixar films and struggled not to
cry while watching *Onward*. I suppose they just disguise
their emotional manipulation a bit better than *BGT*.

I got myself into a bit of trouble while I was filming in
Bosnia. Skender told me about an archaeologist called
Sam Osmanagich who claimed he was excavating the old-
est pyramid on Earth in the hills of Visoko. We decided
this would be a great thing to cover for the show. I met
Sam at the entrance to the pyramid. He had discovered
this structure many years ago and with the help of volunteers and students he was excavating a whole network of
tunnels that would eventually lead to them reactivating
what he believes is some sort of energy beacon. He was
engaging company and I was happy to listen to his tour for
the three hours we were with him despite deciding I
thought it was all bollocks about five minutes into it. It just
seemed so mad to me. He was telling me he was excavating all these existing tunnels, but it looked very much like
he was just digging tunnels. He would also occasionally
show me these huge boulders and ask me to touch them to
feel the energy coursing through my system. I felt nothing, but it wasn't the boulders that sealed the deal for me.
What settled it for me was when I asked him what he
thought had made the tunnels and the pyramid. He
explained it might either be aliens or inner terrestrials, a

race of people who lived underground. It felt unlikely that this theory would hold up under scrutiny.

When I asked the director and producer about what best to say, they asked me to be honest, and so I was, explaining that I felt there might be some holes in his theories. I did also say that I hoped his theory was correct, but I suspected he was going to discover it wasn't before being set upon by all his volunteers.

After the show went out, Skender got in touch with me to tell me he had bumped into Sam, who was very angry with me for what I had said and declared he would never let the BBC film with him ever again. I would therefore like to take this opportunity to apologize to the BBC and to all of you if he is right and I have screwed up. I would also like to take this chance to apologize to the underground people if they exist and I look forward to being executed to set an example to other non-believers. I imagine Sam will have my head mounted in his underground palace.

Despite the fact that a Bosnian archaeologist wants me dead, I have found all these experiences hugely enriching. This is, of course, unhelpful in many ways because I am extremely privileged to have done the things I've done. But I'm convinced that everyone can benefit from going off the beaten track once or twice, as it really does change your outlook on things. What you have to ask yourself, however, is whether you should take the advice of a man who, despite all his banging on about travel, has once again chosen to take his family on holiday to Portugal next year.

Disagreeing with Friends

If you have children, or actually even if you don't, you have a finite number of nights to spend socially. That sounds like I'm morbidly totting up the number of nights you have in your life, which as I type it now sounds like a sensible thing to do when you're making decisions about how to spend your time, but I'm talking more about on a week-to-week basis. Work and family and exhaustion mean that as you get older, you become more selective about what you do with your precious free time. I have written about cancellation ecstasy, but here I'm talking about the occasions when you have managed to get past that block and feel inclined to follow through with your plans to see people.

So the other night we were having a drink with another couple. If you're in a relationship, the decision to spend an evening with another couple, something I would describe as on the lowest rung of the ladder of social engagements, is still a tricky one. One of you always likes them more than the other, and given my wife is usually the one making the arrangements, we tend to see her friends more than mine. In some cases, that's fine. But we've all been in situations where one half of the other couple is a bit of a prick despite having a lovely partner (though I would argue that if somebody has a partner who is a bit of a prick, either they haven't figured out how to extricate themselves, or they have some undercover arsehole tendencies themselves). Prick fragments aside, I find that whole double-date environment a bit nerve-racking. Often you will be asked a question about you as a couple or as a family, and then one of you has to answer on behalf of the team. If you're speaking and your other half is next to you, you have no idea if they're doing an agreeing face or looking at you incredulously and burning a hole in the side of your head.

I have lost count of the number of times we have been asked something like, 'So how are the boys doing at school?', and I've stepped in immediately to answer, thanks to a deep-seated fear of everyone thinking I work too much and am therefore an absent father and completely unaware of what's happening with my children. As I'm talking, I realize I'm very much out of my depth and the far better option would have been to let Leesa speak and then nod aggressively and say 'Absolutely' when she had finished.

Instead, what happens is that Leesa lets me finish, says something like 'How the fuck would you know?', and then I sit and listen to them roast me about how pathetic my fumbling response had been to watch. It's humiliating, but I suppose the plus side is that I've provided a new topic for conversation.

The other thing I have become paranoid about is talking over Leesa. I always find a man talking over his partner a horribly offensive thing to watch, and when I see it, I immediately make plans to try to avoid us having to witness it again. Recently, however, Leesa and I were doing a

Facebook Live, which is essentially us talking shit for half an hour, when one of the comments from the viewers was, 'Are you going to let Leesa get a word in edgeways?' I was immediately mortified. Am I one of those guys? I wanted to respond that Leesa was a little bit nervous about doing the Lives and so I was talking more to help her through it, but that sounds exactly like the sort of thing a bolshie bloke who talked all over his wife would say. I asked Leesa for her take on it but I couldn't be bothered to listen to her response.

On this particular evening of drinking with friends – a couple we both like, no pricks in sight – I had made no such cock-ups, and we were having a nice time. It was at this point that the woman of the other couple expressed a concern about the fact that refugees were coming to the country despite not really having a good enough reason to do so. Now, I disagree with this viewpoint, and actually find it slightly annoying, but please do not worry. I am not going to break down my reasons for that here and now.

I would also make the point that if you disagree with me, and agree with the woman we were out with, that doesn't make us enemies. I do not want you to stop reading this book and stop engaging with what I do. There seems to be this increasing belief that having different opinions on things somehow makes you opponents on everything, which I wholeheartedly disagree with. Don't get me wrong: if somebody thinks that the white man is the superior race and all others should be subservient to them, then I am probably going to struggle to go to their stag do, but in the main, I am happy to accept that my friends and I don't agree on every issue, despite the fact that when an argument I vehemently disagree with is voiced by someone, I momentarily want to smash them in the face.

Piers Morgan typifies this paradox. He is somebody who has recently gone from being the right-wing's darling, when he was moaning about vegan sausage rolls and transitioning snowflakes, to a voice of reason holding the government to account for their Covid-19 failures and even supporting the pulling down of the statue of the slave trader Edward Colston in Bristol. People have been confused, saying things like, 'I can't believe I'm starting to like Piers Morgan!' What that means is that you like the man now that he is expressing views that sit in alignment with your own. It is possible, however, that he has always been a nice man who has said some things you disagree with, or he has always been an utter prick who now happens to agree with you. I will not comment on my take.

When our friend expressed this opinion on refugees, I faced a choice: to counter with my own view, or to nod and say, 'Yes, sure.' There is no danger to the second option, apart from the fact that somebody now thinks you agree with the sentiment. The option to counter with your own view is fraught with risk and creates a confrontation. The idea that you will enter into a healthy discussion that will transfix the four of you before you declare, 'What a spirited discussion! Thank you so much for the opportunity to do a bit of mental sparring!' is pure fantasy. What is far more likely to happen is that you will become annoyed that the other person is not accepting your point of view, you will argue more passionately, never accepting that you might not have the last word, and then your wife will spend the journey home explaining how you went a bit far. I imagine.

Now more than ever we are being encouraged to express our opposition to injustice and inequality on social media, and that silence implies complicity. While you can argue about the merits of that idea all day long, what cannot be denied, and what I have finally accepted, is that no real good can come from an impassioned argument with friends, unless of course you are actually looking to permanently cut them off with a flourish, in which case you can shout, 'Refugees are people too!', throw a drink in their face, storm out and never see them again. I didn't do this, but definitely fantasized about it later.

Don't Let Your Mum Use Zoom

It was the third week of rehearsals for the Lockdown edition of *The Ranganation*. The production team, Zeppotron, had been desperately trying to get the technology working so that by the time we got to the show, it would feel like an actual television show rather than a narcissist in a garage on a Zoom call (which is essentially what it was).

The Ranganation is a show where I talk through the week's issues with twenty members of the public and a couple of celeb guests. My mum is also part of the show, and during rehearsals we had not been able to get her sound to work. Every time I spoke to her it was quiet and muffled, and it was a huge problem because she is such a great part of the show. I cannot tell you how much I enjoyed jokingly calling the man who had been doing shopping for her during lockdown a pervert, much to her dismay. Mainly because she thought he might stop doing her shopping.

At the end of the rehearsal the director asked my mum where she had positioned the microphone they had sent her, at which point she cheerfully pointed out that she hadn't bothered to put it on. The director, with more politeness than she had any reason to use, suggested that she might put on the microphone that had had to be delivered specially by a man dressed like the people at the end of *E.T.* Mum duly placed the microphone on her lapel and the sound instantly became crystal-clear.

When the show went out, Mum and I were due to do an interview on Zoom for *BBC South East*. We had both been sent the link, and my agent, Flo, had spoken to my mum, who confirmed that she had been using Zoom a lot and it wouldn't be a problem for her to get on to the meeting. The time of the meeting arrived and I logged on to the chat to find we were all present except my mum. I called Mum who, rather than using the meeting details sent to her, had started her own meeting at which she was the only attendee and was, I assume, expecting us to find it through hacking or some kind of telepathy. My mum asked me to FaceTime her and I proceeded to talk her through the process of going into her email and clicking on the link provided. As she was doing this, her laptop died. We then decided to use her phone for the interview, which she did but for some reason she couldn't get the audio to work. This left me trying to fix it with her over FaceTime and staring at the inner workings of her ear as she held the phone up to the side of her head.

I had my head in my hands throughout this whole experience as I became increasingly stressed about the delay, which was making me late for something I had to do straight after. What I had forgotten was that I was still on Zoom at my end, and very much on camera and visible to the BBC team, who came on to the line and said, 'Are you OK, Romesh? You seem a little bit flustered.'

I was. Few things will send you into a blind rage quicker

than parents and their inability to operate technology. But I was biting my tongue, and my mum was trying her best. She has been unbelievable through everything that has been asked of her. I joke about how she loves being on TV and getting recognized and all of that is true, but she has never, in all the time she has been asked to do anything, ever said no, or that she would rather not. She came to Sri Lanka to film with me, she spent six weeks in America with me, she has appeared on countless panel shows with me, and has turned up to film as part of *The Ranganation* every week. I ask a lot of my mum, and she always does it willingly and is always brilliant. The very fact that she agreed to do a TV interview on Zoom was amazing in itself, but I just wish she'd admitted that she didn't have a clue how it worked.

I have always had a hang-up about my relationship with my mum, and a deep-rooted fear that I take her for granted and don't do anywhere near enough for her. I certainly help her when I can, and if she ever needs anything I am there, but I worry that I don't see her or speak to her often enough, and in the past I've certainly been guilty of not taking enough of an interest in her life. That was something that hit home when my father died, which made me realize we have a finite amount of time with our parents and have to make the most of it. We have to celebrate them for who they are, and appreciate them while we can. Now, my mum isn't dying or anything – but I do try to make the most of our relationship.

We all make jokes about getting on the phone to our mums and being bored or not engaging with what they're banging on about, and I have been guilty of that in the past. I spent years and years listening to my mum on the phone relive all of her issues with my father. She wouldn't be slagging him off, more lamenting how upset she was at various things that had happened in their marriage. I used to wish she'd stop going on about it, but I have since realized that I am grateful to hear my mum talk about anything. Those moments are precious. I will, of course, tell her not to dwell on the past, and I'm the first to tell her when she's droning on, but I love sitting and listening to her talk about how her neighbour told her that her hair looked nice or she thinks the shirt I was wearing on something or other made me look like an old man.

She also has a longstanding habit of coming up with remedies. Every week she will have read about something we should be doing every day to stay healthy or lose weight, and will relay it to me and my brother. She always forgets the origins of the advice and so every lifestyle tip starts with the vague 'They say you should . . .' Recently my mum has become obsessed with me getting a six-pack. She is convinced that more people will enjoy watching me on TV if I have a clearly defined set of abs 'like Jamie and Freddie' – Redknapp and Flintoff, my co-stars on *A League Of Their Own*, with whom my mum has developed an unhealthy obsession.

I asked her how she expected me to manage it, considering my body shape is borderline offensive, I have zero willpower when it comes to eating and I lack the genetics required to make any of it happen. My mum then informed me: 'They say you can do it easily if you watch what you eat and have turmeric.' Now, I am fully on board with the benefits of turmeric, but if scientists had found a way to use turmeric to overcome the near-impossible odds that most of us face when trying to achieve a six-pack, I'm pretty sure I wouldn't have had to wait until a phone call from my mum to find out. A woman who has been on the 'turmeric plan' for a while now and does not seem to be obviously progressing to a defined set of abdominals. Fortunately, I should add, because, much as I love her, I would find the sight of my mum with a six-pack genuinely disturbing.

I suppose what this is supposed to lead to is a neat conclusion where I say that I have realized how I feel about technology and my mum is probably how my children feel about me and the same, and my appreciation for my relationship with my mother means that I actually cherish the times spent talking her through how to complete a Face-Time call. The truth is, though, I have seen about as much of her chin in close-up on a video call as I can possibly take.

Be Careful with Hot Sauce

I have to be honest, this chapter is pretty disgusting. It paints me in the most unattractive light and is possibly the worst thing I have ever divulged. Just so you know, after you read this next bit, you'll probably think that I have shared too much information and you will never look at me in the same way again. I apologize. But shit happens.

I have always been obsessed with hot sauce. It's something that was instilled in me at childhood. In our house, our 'ketchup' was West Indian Hot Pepper Sauce, which my dad would put on absolutely everything. I soon fell in love with the taste and followed suit, regularly getting carried away and ruining meals by adding too much. Some days the ratio has hit 1:1 sauce to food, which even for the keenest of hot sauce connoisseurs is far too much. There have definitely been occasions when I've had to throw away my dinner because I have doused it to the point of rendering it completely inedible. From a young age, I also became very good at adding it to things that really had no place being fiery hot. My mum was in on it too. She used to make a pasta bake, but would reinforce stereotypes by adding so much hot sauce that a visitor joining us for dinner would be forgiven for thinking we were trying to poison them, or at least deter them from coming round again.

Hot pepper sauce is so ingrained in my system that it has become a trigger for me. If I am away from home and have some, I am immediately thrown into the warm nostalgia of growing up and eating with my parents. So much so that I have considered keeping a bottle of it in my luggage. I have lost count of the number of meals I have eaten on the road that would have been improved by hot sauce. I only changed my mind when it occurred to me that somebody who carries an emergency bottle of hot sauce around with them at all times probably has his priorities wrong. It is difficult to argue that you are not a greedy person when one of the things that you consider an essential item is a condiment. I am also highly allergic to bee stings and am supposed to carry adrenaline with me. I don't do that, because I seemingly don't give as much of a shit about protecting my life as I do protecting myself against under-seasoned food.

This might all seem relatively harmless, but the side effect of a rampant hot sauce addiction is the unfortunate effect it has on your digestive system. I'm pretty certain that over the years I've managed to dissolve my stomach lining. Even now, several times a year I am liable to basically render myself out of commission by eating too much hot food the previous day. It is unbearable. And it catches you by surprise. I have often been heading into work on the train feeling totally fine and then realizing I am seconds away from shitting myself. I then have to decide whether I am going to try and hold it until I find a decent toilet, or do one of the worst things any human can do – shit on a train. Shitting on a train is such an awful, life-changing trauma that I think there should be some sort of counselling service set up for people who have been forced to do it. It is so horrific, particularly when it's an emergency shit, which I would argue it has to be if you arc on a train, because who the hell is routinely shitting on a train?! When you finish, you feel initial relief but you are immediately flooded with fear. You realize that everyone in the carriage knows that you've been in there a while and have just committed an atrocity. Do you brazenly step out of the cubicle and walk back to your seat with everyone staring at you? What if the door doesn't shut after you, essentially letting the carriage know that you are a fucking animal? Worst of all, someone might be standing outside waiting to use the toilet immediately after you, in which case you simply have to jump out of the window.

It's only recently that I've started tempering what I eat to avoid these situations, which I see as both a sign of ageing and a revelation. For the first time in my life I have found myself going to put hot sauce on my food and then thinking, 'Do you really want to cry on a train tomorrow?' and measuring out a more conservative amount. Occasionally I still think, 'Let's just roll the dice.' I go for it anyway and then the next day I'm on a steel throne in carriage 4.

I'm ashamed to say that this problem has become so prevalent that my wife will sometimes be my chilli eyes. She sees me sitting down with a bottle of hot sauce and says, 'That's the third meal today you've had hot sauce with. Don't you think you should take it easy?' While it's nice of her to keep an eye on me, I also find it profoundly depressing. What is essentially happening there is my wife is saying, 'I have been monitoring your shitting situation and actually think I need to intervene for your own sake.'

Just as I was starting to get a handle on things, I discovered a new hot sauce. It's made by Mark Gevaux, who is famous as the West Ham ribman. All his hot sauces happen to be vegan. He makes a hot sauce called Holy Fuck which is hotter than the sauce I normally use, but is so tasty you don't even particularly notice how hot it is. It is absolutely delicious. More recently, however, he has started making a variety called Bacon Holy Fuck, which might be the best condiment on the planet. It is fiercely addictive, and I recently bought a two-litre bottle of it, which now means that I essentially view all my meals as a hot-sauce-delivery system. There is a moral dilemma here for the vegan, of course, because Mark sells a lot of meat, and the most carnivore of meats: ribs. However, as it turns out, I am less judgy when the sauce is delicious.

A few days ago I had a particularly saucy day, adding it to every one of my meals, even taking a moment to think about whether it would go well on toast. The next morning I was having a bit of a phone mooch in bed next to Leesa, when all of a sudden my internal systems went into overdrive. I was in emergency shit town, and even the toilet that was about ten steps away didn't seem close enough. I sprinted to it and, without getting into too much disgusting detail, I was there for 45 minutes. When I eventually emerged, my wife was sat up in bed. I assume she had spent the last three-quarters of an hour rehearsing the different ways in which she was going to say, 'I told you so.' She said, 'I think today maybe eat some plainer stuff? That sounded bad.' That sounded bad! She heard what was happening. The first thing that she experienced in the morning was the sound of her 'lover' delivering seven shades of hell in the en suite.

It has occurred to me that there must be a point at which you just cannot find your partner attractive or sexy any more, and I would argue hearing them dealing with the hot sauce craps is right up there as a key tipping point. I don't even have the advantage of good looks to offset the ensuing repulsion. I imagine that if you heard Ryan Gosling curling out a spicy one you'd think twice. Maybe.

I have no idea what I'm trying to offer as wisdom from this, to be honest. I guess take from it what you will – be careful with hot sauce, try to keep the magic alive, or just soundproof your toilet.

Don't Get Too Comfortable

I think there's a strong possibility that Leesa and I have got too comfortable. I mean, it's nice being comfortable. But it does sometimes occur to me that maybe we are too settled in our relationship. (I should point out that I'm fully aware I've just revealed that my wife has to monitor my hot sauce intake, which most definitely makes her uncomfortable, but does nothing to help us on a romantic level.) I don't know how other couples manage their level of mystique. When you first get together with someone, it's giddy and amazing because you are getting to know them and finding out about who they are and it's all either incredibly exciting or they reveal something about themselves that you find unacceptable and you split up.

Leesa and I could not know more about each other. There are no surprises left any more. I have become so comfortable with Leesa that I've even been known to comment to her on the attractiveness of other women, forgetting who I'm talking to. Leesa remains utterly unbothered by this. That is either a sign that she is so comfortable and in love with me that she recognizes this is simply me being open and honest with her, or she is storing up these incidents to give to a lawyer at some point in the future.

I feel similarly, though there was a time when I was, I admit, quite a jealous person. I would be in a relationship and if the girl I was seeing was chatting to another guy or talking about a guy being attractive, I would find that threatening. I remember working at Gatwick airport. A girl I was dating was working at one of the other shops, and we had arranged for me to go and have a quick chat before I headed home after my shift. I went over to her and she was chatting to some guy she worked with. I sat down and said hello to both of them and it became clear that he was going to be staying for the duration. I was silently pissed off and got up and walked away.

Later on that day, she phoned me and said, 'You won't believe this – that guy thought you might be jealous or upset by the fact he was talking to me. I told him you just weren't like that.' I laughed and said, 'That's mad,' deciding against telling her that I had in fact spent the afternoon creating an effigy of him just so I could smash the shit out of it, and that if I had the right sort of connections I would have arranged a hit on the prick.

I don't know where that kind of jealousy comes from. Part of it is from being a young male with testosterone oozing from every pore (now evaporated). But part of it comes from some pretty deep-seated insecurity. I remember walking over and seeing that guy who, to my mind, was much better suited to my girlfriend than me. He was good-looking, charming, and if I had been the person responsible for setting her up with someone, I definitely would have preferred him to me.

Another girl I was seeing went travelling with friends

and met a group of guys while away. When they came back to the UK they arranged a night out, to which I was invited. I remember seeing the blokes at this night out and immediately thinking they were much more the type of guy I could see my girlfriend with, and actually maybe it would be for the best if she ended up with one of them. I even went as far as planning the chat in my head, where I was prepared for her to tell me she liked one of them, and then I would be super gracious about how I wanted the best for her, and an R'n'B song called 'See You Next Lifetime' would play and I would walk off into the distance.

I don't seem to have that problem with Leesa, and sometimes I wonder if that's a bad sign. Similarly, I don't know what it would take for Leesa to feel any kind of jealousy about me. This might be because of our inbuilt trust of one another, but I have started to think it might be laziness. The other day Leesa and I were discussing how, if we ever did split up, we might decide to continue living together anyway, both to save admin and because we couldn't be bothered to find another partner.

I do find it unbelievable when I hear about people leaving their partners of twenty years for someone else. Putting the energy into seeing someone new and impressing them in a dating scenario seems like such an impossible effort. I genuinely couldn't be arsed. Even the idea of taking my top off in front of someone new fills me with dread. I mean, I'm not buzzing about the bottoms coming off either. The whole package is a nightmare, to be honest.

Then again, after so many years together, it is incredible that you still manage to find things to talk about, isn't it?

This has been brought into sharp focus by our experience of lockdown, which I suppose has been a preview of what life is like in retirement. You're no longer generating separate experiences so you have nothing new to say to each other, unless you can come up with something sparkling that happened in the bathroom. The level of what you think is worth sharing drops rapidly. Leesa came home after a walk to tell me she thought she had seen a fox but it was in fact a cat. And that was the end of the story.

I sometimes wonder how any couple survives, when you inevitably get to a point where you have heard each other's stories numerous times and are bored to death by them. It's exciting when you have a banger anecdote that the group you are with haven't heard, but it's also terrible for your other half who has to watch you go through the motions of it once again, perhaps even noticing little changes and alterations you made to make it funnier, each time moving it away from the original truth, until one day they are listening to you recount the story at a wedding and they suddenly scream, 'That's not even what fucking happened any more!'

Maybe getting to that stage of boredom, of comfort, of being fully saturated in someone else's life, is entirely the point. I, for one, am not sure about this obsession with keeping things spicy in a relationship. The idea is that to give a partnership longevity, one or both of you have to make an ongoing effort to keep things surprising and new, and essentially to simulate what the relationship was like at the beginning when you were trying to impress each other and hadn't morphed into your disgusting, warts-and-all true selves.

I understand the appeal of that. You are not farting in front of each other. You go out on mad evenings all the time with surprise romantic experiences. You'll be sat at home ready to watch an episode of *Tiger King*, and your other half will say something like, 'Forget *Tiger King*, I'm going to show you the real thing,' and you jump in a car and you're on your way to late-night dinner at a safari park, looking out at all the animals, before retiring to your private suite for some lovemaking that is less out of choice and more of an obligation because they have gone to so much effort.

I understand the appeal of that, and I realize I run the risk of many of you contacting my wife to tell her to get the fuck out of our relationship, but is it so wrong to actually really enjoy just sitting and watching *Tiger King*? I mean, it's easier, isn't it? Plus there's always the bonus for Leesa that I might fall asleep before the end of the show and so she doesn't have to touch me.

Don't get me wrong – it is nice to go out for dinner and do romantic things, and Leesa and I do have date nights, but I don't necessarily prefer that to staying in. I like sitting and having a drink while quietly watching a show, with occasional moments to talk about what an absolute lunatic Joe Exotic is. I like the fact that sometimes we are honest and say we can't be arsed to do anything tonight and we just read books next to each other. These are all nice comfortable things, and I hope that Leesa feels the same way, although it is possible she is secretly plotting her escape from this loveless prison throughout every hour of Netflix.

Also, you don't always have to be talking all the time, although this is something I have only recently come to appreciate. There was a time when we would go out for dinner and survey the other couples sitting in silence, and we would smugly scoff at how their relationships had died and how we would never allow ourselves to fall into that level of despair.

We have realized one or two things since then: either those couples have reached a point where they don't need to be constantly talking because they are at peace with each other and completely in love, or Leesa and I are in deep shit because we are now doing exactly the same thing. I would much prefer sitting in silence to constantly jabbering away to fill all the gaps, but it does look tragic, doesn't it? When you see a couple having dinner, and each course arrives and they eat it in silence, the only animated conversation taking place when they are talking to the waiter. Is that comfort or the beginning of the end? Because Leesa and I do occasionally make shit small talk at dinner to avoid facing the very real possibility that we may need to get a divorce.

It is undoubtedly the case, however, that with the comfort and love of a long-term relationship, there is also erosion of mystique. I know we're supposed to accept each other warts and all, but I am not convinced this is the best way to ensure longevity. Maybe you don't need to spice things up in the bedroom, or plan over-the-top surprises, but it's always a good idea to maintain some boundaries. For example, just the other night I was pulling off my boxer shorts before bed, and I got my toe stuck in one of the legs and had a little tumble. Now, obviously, not the worst thing that's ever happened, but I am almost certain that as my wife looked across at me to see my penis and gelatinous belly jiggle up and down as I frantically hopped to try and regain balance, I heard her sexual organs pull their main off switch. What I am saying is, I think it is for the good of the relationship if, no matter how close and in love you are, you get changed in separate rooms. While we're on the subject, I also think it's absolutely unacceptable to walk into a bathroom when someone is having a shower. To prevent this, I've always locked the bathroom door. Leesa asked me why I was doing that, obviously suspecting me of having some sort of wank session, so I started leaving it unlocked to avoid arousing suspicion. I then find myself in the middle of a shower when Leesa walks in to discuss whether we need a new television, just as I am really going to town on my arse crack. Now, I am not embarrassed to say that I like this area to be spotless. The cleansing ritual is as thorough as it is vigorous. What it isn't, is suitable for spectators. So I didn't appreciate her wandering in, able to do so because of her request for me to leave the door unlocked, before running out again in cackling horror.

Comfort is wonderful, but it could do with a little more bloody privacy.

Role Model

If you think you're a brilliant dad, I don't know that you are fully aware of how complicated this shit is. We are all just muddling along, trying not to damage them too much. The other day I walked into the living room and went to pretend-punch my son, who was on the sofa. Unfortunately I misjudged it and punched him square in the leg, which made him cry. I felt absolutely awful. I looked up at my wife who had essentially just watched her husband walk into the living room and punch her child. It was horrendous, though I would argue strongly that my son was milking it. He knows I have a track record of offering rewards to bring periods of trauma to an end, and what this has done is encourage the kids to exaggerate any mishaps in the hope of further extortion.

My kids are very loving but they also take the piss. I have no idea where they've picked that up. Could it be that my wife and I are constantly roasting each other and now the house is filled with quipping twats? You cannot say anything without someone finding a way to turn it back on you. They have also started reviewing what I'm doing. Last night, Leesa ordered the kids to bed and one of the boys said he didn't want to go. I replied, 'Oh, you don't want to go to bed? Well, in that case, don't worry about it. We didn't realize.' I was being sarcastic and funny. Or so I thought. But my eldest son immediately said, 'Er, Dad, you've used that joke a few times now – it's getting a bit old.' He had basically become Twitter.

One of my deepest paranoias is about getting things wrong with my kids. Every hour of every day is a series of opportunities to damage them in some way. We went away on a romantic break recently, which paradoxically involved taking our children. Leesa doesn't like being away from the kids, which is both because she misses them too much and because she wants to reduce the chances that we might end up having sex. I pretend I'm disappointed about that but to be honest most of the time I'm too exhausted to scrape together the energy to even try it on.

Our eldest son is getting to the point where he doesn't want to be doing the same things as the other two. The three of them together can be best described as a terrible party you can't leave. At the hotel, the younger boys wanted to go and do 'kids' club' but he wanted to go for a bike ride, so I agreed to take him.

This represents a series of issues for me, as does doing anything remotely physical with the kids, mainly because I am shit at it. I work with Freddie Flintoff and Jamie Redknapp on *A League Of Their Own*, and their kids are involved with sport at a high level. I shouldn't even practise sport with my kids because their very exposure to my level of skill would set their bar far too low. They would grow up thinking it was impressive to do two keepy-ups before running round the garden in celebration at overcoming your coordination issues. I find the whole thing bloody humiliating. We often take the kids to the park to play football, and I am struck by how much better other dads are with their children – doing drills, pinging long shots in the air for their kids to bring down. What we do is put some jumpers down and kick a ball very short distances between us before missing the goal repeatedly. Fortunately for them, Leesa is actually athletic and coordinated, and so I pray they have inherited some sports prowess from her. On the other hand, I do wonder if that might be even more embarrassing, as we head down to the park for the four of them to ritually humiliate me.

Recently we were playing down the park when a family walked past and their little kid asked to join in. I had no idea this was allowed. If I was walking past some people playing a game, my instinct would be to walk as far away from the game as possible for fear of the ball coming to me.

Anyway, it became clear why this family thought it was OK. It was because this boy was absolutely incredible. I stood and watched this kid run rings around my entire family. He was back-heeling, he was doing maze runs, he even nutmegged Leesa, which to be fair I found enjoyable. I was supposed to be playing as well, but I kind of dipped out, partly because I didn't want to accidentally injure him, but mainly because I didn't want to be made to look like an idiot by this little show-off.

I'm pretty sure that family take that kid around different parks, releasing him into games and watching him destroy the self-esteem and confidence of anybody else playing. After watching this child single-handedly destroy

Ranganathan United, his parents called him off and they walked out of our lives. I looked at my family in utter disbelief as they talked about how much fun that was. I was minded to give them a team talk about having such a lack of winning mentality that they thought a shit-kicking was a fun experience, but I judged the room and decided against it.

It was for these reasons that I was wary about taking our son for a bike ride. I hadn't ridden a bike in a long time, and saw this as yet another chance for our kids' ever decreasing respect for me to be eroded further. I often wonder if it's possible that they have 'father envy', seeing other dads being amazing and supportive and athletic, and then looking across at me wheezing my way through a round of crazy golf, and dreaming about a paternity test that unmasks me as an impostor.

We borrowed bikes from the hotel and while my son was putting on his helmet, I had a quick ride around the car park because I was pretty sure I could be the first person in history who actually forgot how to ride a bike.

We headed off on our bikes together, with me starting to feel a sense of achievement that this is what fathers and sons are supposed to do. Arguably, it was embarrassing that this was the first time it had happened, but to be fair to me, my dad never went on a bike ride with me either. In fact, as I'm typing this, I realize I've never seen either of my parents on a bike. Is that weird? I don't even know if they could/can ride bikes. That was just an aside and now I've become obsessed by it. I'm strongly considering going to my mum's house now and demanding she give me some sort of demonstration.

We rode along the path for a while and arrived at what looked like the woodland bike trail. The first thing that had occurred to me since setting out is how much faster a bike feels when you're an adult. My recollection of being a kid was just hammering the thing as quickly as possible, never able to get it to go fast enough. Now, riding along at a leisurely pace felt like a near-death experience.

We rode into the woods and I started absolutely shitting it. The bike was smashing through this bumpy trail at what felt like 90mph and at one point I took off into the air, which I found terrifying. Then I looked across to my son, who was keeping up with me and holding back from over-taking. It didn't look like he was going fast at all. It was at that point that I realized I had become a pussy.

This threw up a whole new set of issues. Being irrationally scared of riding a bike is something that is fine for me to live with, but I did not want this to infect my son. One of the biggest pressures of being a parent is that you are acting as a role model for your kids, and whether they claim to find you embarrassing or not, they are learning what is acceptable from your behaviour. What I didn't want was for my son to think it was normal for riding a bike in the woods to make you cry.

It may be the PTSD that makes me remember this as particularly anxiety-inducing, partly because of the speed, but mainly because I was desperately trying to look completely unbothered by it. I kept looking at him and smiling and saying unconvincing things like, 'This is fun, right?' and he would nod, genuinely loving it.

After a few hundred trainer-killing metres on the trail,

we came to a series of gates we would have to carry our bikes over if we were to continue the ride. I didn't want to do that. I didn't even want to ride back. I wanted to discuss the possibility of abandoning these fucking bikes completely. But I also wanted to make my son happy, and not damage him through exposure to my insanity, and so I explained that I was going to jump over the gate and he could pass his bike to me.

It was at that point he said to me, 'Dad, can we just go back?'

My son. My lovely son. My beautiful lovely gorgeous smart clever son. Yes. Yes, we can go back! Thank you!! Thank you for bringing this nightmare to an end!

I didn't say any of that. As casually as I could, I said, 'You sure, mate?' He confirmed he was and we headed back.

I have to confess to having mixed feelings about this. Part of me felt happy to have done the bike ride with him and overjoyed that it had come to an end. But there was a part of me that didn't feel as comfortable about us turning around so soon. My big concern was why he had decided he didn't want to carry on. Had he been cursed with my negativity? I had to ask him. I was hoping he'd say something like, 'The conditions just weren't thrilling enough, so I thought, what's the point?' What he actually said was, 'It was way too muddy and it was getting all over my trainers.' He's been cursed.

This may seem like a small incident but, to me, it represents so many of the fears I have as a parent. I don't want my kids to be like me. I want them to be so much better than me. My childhood memories are filled with me being shit at everything. My lack of coordination and excess weight meant that I was the worst in every group at any activity. I had a brief spell from fourteen to about eighteen where I dropped some weight and felt like I could start having a go at stuff but the truth is being thin doesn't make you coordinated.

These early experiences of failure instilled in me a fear of competition that evolved into not wanting to take part in anything. I have no desire to get involved in any activity that has a winner, or rankings, or any kind of league table. That's the thing I hate most about my job. In the entertainment industry you have ratings and reviews where you are compared to other acts and shows and ranked accordingly. When I started doing a podcast I was genuinely upset to discover there was a chart for the ones people are listening to the most.

With our kids now, I don't really know how I feel about the whole concept of competition. I understand why it is seen as a positive thing – because it apparently encourages you to improve, to strive to be better and not to languish in mediocrity. We are constantly being told that competition in schools is being eroded and that kids are given prizes for being crap but for taking part and how disgusting that is because we should be celebrating excellence and so on. I get that, but where you insist on having winners there will always be losers. And in some cases, no amount of ambition and dedication will change the outcome.

I was doing an online spin class recently (and if that isn't an example of how much I have lost sight of my roots, I don't know what is), when the instructor started talking about how working out is all about hustle and willpower and grinding and pushing yourself, and that he came from nothing but didn't let that stop him, and he carried on pushing and pushing and eventually got to where he is now. Which is all very impressive, and I have the utmost respect for him, but I wish he would also acknowledge that it took him a shit ton of luck as well. I find this increasingly widespread propaganda that we are all where we are because of what we have put into it utterly infuriating. There are people who would have been better than that instructor at doing what he does but he had the benefit of good fortune. There are many people who would have been better at doing every single aspect of the job I do but I've had the lucky breaks.

Social media is the most guilty of pushing this bullshit. So many people on Instagram will post about their humble beginnings and how they can't believe where they've got to and people will affirm their fuckwittery by commenting, 'Well done. You are an inspiration!' I can't believe that nobody is going, 'Hey, listen, I am having a shit time of things and to be honest this really feels like you're rubbing your good fortune in my fucking face.'

Which leaves you with the question of how to bring up your children with the best possible chances of being happy, and if that is even the best thing to aim for. I do want my children to be happy, but not if that means they are ignorant of the issues and inequalities and general shit that's going on. I want them to engage with all of that. But also be happy. Which feels a bit impossible. So in reality, what we have decided to do is stop pretending we have a plan, take each decision as it comes and hope to God they figure it out for themselves in some way, or at least not realize that we hadn't properly prepared them for life until after we're dead.

Look After Your Health

My wife is obsessed with the boys being healthy. I say obsessed, by which I mean she actually makes an effort to think about what they eat, whereas I would happily feed them Doritos and biscuits all day – largely because they love it and it makes me feel like a great parent to see them so happy, though what I take to be excitement at spending time with their father is in all likelihood sugar-induced hyperactivity.

Just recently, the weekly shop hasn't managed to stretch the whole week. I would argue that Leesa forgets we are a household of five. Because of her fear of wasting food, she tends to order the bare minimum, and for reasons I don't quite understand she chooses to ignore the things I like. I've lost count of the number of times Marmite has been missed off the shopping list. I don't understand the need to wait until Marmite has run out to buy more – that only means you are going to have a period of having no Marmite at all, which can lead to stress. Much better to buy a jar a week so that your anxiety levels are reduced by knowing there is always Marmite to hand if you need it. As I see it, you might as well stockpile anything that doesn't go off in a few days. Of course there is a valid argument that says,

'Why don't you do the shopping then, you moany prick?' And the answer is I'm not ready for that kind of pressure.

Leesa was brought up very differently to me, and this has resulted in us having very different habits. Leesa wasn't allowed fizzy drinks as a child. All her cereals were sugar-free and her bread had to be the holiest of wholemeal with seeds and bits of branches in. My mum had a much more relaxed attitude to sugar, in that she just loved to see her children eating. What this meant was we had whatever cereals we wanted, our bread was always as white as the girls my mum hoped we'd stay away from (I'm kidding, she didn't want us near *any* girls before 25), and we had a guy who delivered fizzy drinks every week. I'm constantly taking the piss out of Leesa for her much stricter regimen, but she is slim and without a single filling, whereas I have struggled with weight issues my whole life and have more fillings than Krispy Kreme.

Setting out one day to fill our bare cupboards, I decided to ignore Leesa's rules about what we were supposed to have, and bought white bread and a huge box of Coco Pops and as many packets of crisps as I could physically get in the car. I returned home a hero – the kids greeted me at the door with hugs and they cheered as if a goal was being scored every time I unveiled a new item.

It was a bit out of order – my wife, who has kept the boys healthy their whole lives, had to watch me be treated like a World Cup winner by allowing them to believe that treats are good and they should ignore the boring busybodies who say otherwise, regardless of the fact that my side of the family suffers from type-2 diabetes and heart disease.

I have struggled my entire life with my endless greed. I can't imagine that anyone is as greedy as me. I am constantly thinking about food, and even while I'm eating I'm thinking about the next thing I'm going to eat after I finish. We once had a birthday cake in the fridge, from which I took the tiniest of pieces a couple of times as I was walking through the kitchen. I only realized how many times I had done that when my wife went to remove the foil to give the kids some for dessert and it was empty. I then had to explain to the family that I didn't feel sorry at all.

I've been trying intermittent fasting, where you eat for eight hours a day, then fast for sixteen hours. The idea is that your body goes into some sort of ketosis mode when you fast for a time and so you are able to manage your weight more easily. I mean, if you're looking for some sort of science behind the explanation here, then God help you. I've been able to manage this fairly successfully, save for two issues. First, the eight-hour window, which seems to be completely filled with me eating. Because I know I'm permitted to eat in that time and I know I'm going to be fasting, I spend the entirety of those eight hours stuffing my piggy little face. Second, the sixteen-hour window, approaching the end of which I'm so hungry that if somebody even looks at me I am likely to either snap at them or eat them.

I sometimes wonder if Leesa and I are compatible when it comes to meals. She doesn't seem to have greed issues at all, and, more distressingly, she only eats when she is hungry. I find it absolutely maddening. We'll be having a nice lunch and she will say something like, 'Wow, won't need dinner tonight after eating all of this.' What the fuck are you talking about? Why would you ruin a wonderful lunch by putting the idea in my head that we might not be having dinner? I don't understand people who are not thinking about food constantly.

I am often asked by people how I manage to be so chunky despite being a vegan. Vegans are usually very slim, and my terrible shape has on occasion fuelled people's arguments against a vegan diet. I feel slightly embarrassed about that, but it only serves to reassure me that there is no way I can consider abandoning veganism. I can only imagine the size I would balloon to if I was given free rein to eat whatever I like. That I have managed, despite the restrictions of my diet, to stay as overweight as I have, is almost impressive. The truth is, you have to think of these things comparatively. If I wasn't a vegan I would be fucking enormous.

Whenever we go out anywhere, I'm thinking about food. When we go to a theme park, say, Leesa will pipe up about lunch at around 2pm (I mean, what the fuck, man?) and ponder where the food places might be, whereas I am able to list every single food outlet we've passed for the previous four hours. The only thing that stops me getting something from every single one of them is that most of them don't have vegan options, or the vegan option is unappealing. Leesa has recently taken pity on me and started packing snacks, but this might be more to do with the fact that keeping the moaning beast she has chosen to spend her life with full will help her enjoy her day more.

I used to think that you should listen to your body and eat when you are hungry. I was of the opinion that you shouldn't deny yourself for the sake of vanity, and that as long as you exercised a bit and stayed on top of things, you'd be all right, and it might just be that overweight was your natural default setting. But I would also say there is no way my body needs three Magnums in a row, but that is often what I find it craving. I mean, I am just greedy. At that theme park I eventually found a place with veggie hot-dogs and as I ordered one I looked into their storage fridge to see how many they had left because I knew I'd be coming back to get another one at some point.

We all seem to be increasingly health-conscious now, but there's an argument we have confused good health with vanity. What is presented as healthy is not normal. The magazine *Men's Health* will almost exclusively picture a man on the cover with defined abs and shoulders you could lie across. All very desirable, of course, but fuck you for saying that's *Men's Health*. That's *Men's* 'workout twice a day every day and don't eat sugar ever'. I resent that image being held up as a definition of men's health. It simply isn't. I concede, however, that it would be difficult to sell a magazine that featured a regular guy on the front with the tagline: 'Want to look fairly unspectacular but probably not have early onset coronary issues like this guy?'

The decision you have to make is whether the sacrifices required to stay healthy throughout your life are worth the pay-off at the end of it. Is eighty-five years of living as a vegan teetotal non-smoker who exercises regularly better or worse than fifty-five years as a bacon- and ice-cream-eating coke dabbler who only ran once in his life and that was to a kebab shop? Plus, is any of that relevant when it's highly likely you're going to get killed by someone looking at their phone while driving anyway? That is why fitness for vanity is so useful, I guess. We are not long-term enough in our thinking to be able to regulate our behaviour simply in order to live longer. The reward has to be more immediate. You need the added impetus of being able to wear a T-shirt without having a bout of depression.

In addition to my impressive greed, I have a family condition that makes falling ill a lot more likely. I realize this is supposed to be an incentive to minimize the health risks in my life, but it has definitely worked the other way. The most likely outcome for me is that regardless of what I do, I die in twenty years. That is what has happened to most of the men in our family, as our bloodline seems to produce ropey hearts. The only men in my family who look like they are going to buck that trend are those who regularly eat flaxseed, never really go out and, once a month, as a treat, allow themselves to eat something with flavour. I don't value longevity that much. I would have enjoyed *The Last Jedi* a lot more if it was an hour shorter and cut out the casino bit, plus, if I go early doors, it's one less parent for the kids to feel obligated to call at the weekend (there is no way Leesa will stay with me beyond her forties).

I think the key is to find balance, which feels like the most obvious conclusion that anyone has ever come to about anything. As a rule, though, if I now consider a new diet or form of exercise or my mum's latest turmeric remedy, I ask myself the question: 'Is this something you might have a good chance of maintaining for a long time or even for ever?' If it isn't, then I won't do it, which rules out mad diets and crazy exercise regimes. What I do instead is pick more sensible things that I can envisage sticking to while still living my life and enjoying myself.

And then I go and fail at these as well.

Alcohol Abuse

The relationship I have with alcohol is problematic. I don't mean alcoholism, which is a horrible illness, but I do mean that over the years I have found what it does to me and my behaviour horrendous, and I'm frequently reminded that it brings out the worst in everyone.

Almost without exception, every single evening I have had with alcohol has been great to shit in a ratio of about 1:3. It varies in terms of levels of smashed as you get older, but the pattern stays very similar. There is the beginning bit of the evening where you meet up with everyone and you all know that getting drunk is the eventual goal. Conversation is stilted as everyone is really waiting for the drink to kick in, 'banter' to start and inhibitions to disappear.

After that, there is a section of the evening when you are perfectly drunk. You feel a buzz, you are happy, and everyone seems charming and hilarious, and in particular you. You are having the time of your life and can't believe you don't do this every single night. I remember in my twenties, for about two years, there would be a point in every evening where my friends and I would tell each other that we loved each other, and despite the fact that we always did that when we went out on the piss, every time would feel like the first time any of us had said it.

What would be ideal would be if you could keep the evening at that point. If, like a shower hitting its set temperature, you could keep it perfectly in that moderately drunk stage, and spend the rest of the evening not necessarily telling people you love them constantly but sitting in that zone. Sadly I reckon that has only ever happened about three times in my life.

What actually happens is you try to keep that buzz going but take it way too far. Suddenly, you find yourself feeling more and more aggressive, you start making terrible decisions, and the evening ends with you puking up into a recycling bin behind the KFC. One of your friends tries to help you and you tell them this is typical of them and how you've actually never liked them.

I've lost count of the number of times I've made a prick of myself as a result of overdrinking. One night last year, I decided I needed to stop. I didn't make a big show of telling all my friends, I just decided I was going give up the booze and if anyone asked about it I'd pretend I had to do it for work. There are various reasons I decided to stop drinking. One of them was the fact that I seem to think I'm a lot funnier when I'm drunk. My anecdotes get louder, my listening gets rarer, and I essentially become an obnoxious twat.

What's obviously worse is the fear you feel the next morning as you try to recall what you've done. I find it absolutely agonizing. I wake up in the morning and immediately look at my phone to see if I have any texts from people telling me I was a complete arsehole last night. If I don't have any, I text them to ask. That's normally followed by the reply, 'What makes you think that?' Then I am faced with having just given them reason to suspect that I might have been an arsehole in the first place. Also, I'm not sure what answer I'm expecting that would be helpful. I'm argu- ably better off not knowing, unless that behaviour has made me a suspect in an ongoing investigation.

The biggest challenge came the first time Sober Romesh went out with my mates for what was billed as a big night. It was one of those nights where the main aim was to get as smashed as possible. It is arguable that my friends and I are way too old to make this the main object of our evening. I arrived and ordered a Diet Coke, and told the group of raised eyebrows that I wasn't drinking at the moment. One of my friends immediately asked me, 'What's the point of going out with you then?' Then followed an hour and a half of them trying to convince me to start drinking.

'Why are you being so bloody boring?'

'You're not funny when you're sober!'

That reads like they were being abusive, which I sup- pose they were, but the truth is they were just encouraging me to have a good time. And on a night when getting drunk was the ultimate goal I suppose I was being quite boring. Fortunately they soon got pissed enough to forget I was even there.

British culture isn't kind to people who decide to give up drinking. When you announce to a group of people that you don't drink or have decided to stop drinking, you have to defend your position much as though you had just announced you have started to enjoy punching puppies.

They will also not accept the decision unless you were an alcoholic or committed an atrocity. 'I just don't understand why you can't have one drink. You just beat someone up. He's probably breathing normally again by now! And he'll be enjoying a beer.' Another weird thing to get used to is that normally, when you are drinking, you start an evening anticipating it getting better as it goes on. When you are a non-drinker with a group of drinkers, you start the evening with the conversation being as good as it's going to get. For many of my evenings sober, about midway through the evening I would start trying to figure out the earliest point at which I could leave. You know how when you go out to a bar and you're drinking, at some stage you'll look at your watch and wonder where the evening has gone? When you're not drinking, the evening becomes an endless vortex in which an hour feels like six months. I'd go so far as to say it's worse than the wait to rinse hair dye out.

What I discovered was that any evening with your friends that involves alcohol doesn't need to go on after 10 p.m. Because after 10 p.m. no new conversation happens. You essentially listen to remixes of the earlier conversations over and over again. I've spent my life thinking I hang out with a group of people who are funny and witty and hugely entertaining. After spending one evening with them while sober, I ended the night believing I hang out with a bunch of complete and utter fuckwits, and that I might be better deliberately fuckwitting myself with booze so I can join in.

This isn't true, of course. The fact is that no matter how engaging you are while sober, alcohol turns you into a tosser. I think it's the combination of the lack of an edit function along with an increased belief in how entertaining you are. This presents a problem, of course, for the sober participant. How do you continue to hang around with your friends, knowing you will never enjoy the latter part of the evening, and in fact might end up disliking them more and more? What are you supposed to do? Set up a separate group of friends who sit around drinking Appletiser and talking about how uncouth our alcohol-drinking friends have become? I'm being facetious, but the truth is, when you stop drinking, you suddenly realize how centred around alcohol your social life is. What I didn't want to do was to encourage any of them to stop drinking with me, like some sort of Dry January zealot. I think that would have tipped them over the edge. They were already suspicious enough of me as it was, what with me being a vegan. Regardless of how long we have been hanging out together, me being a teetotal vegan was probably enough to get me kicked out of the group.

I feel like I might be being unfair on my friends here. Whenever we meet up it's always a laugh, but when you are the only non-drinker you feel a little bit like you are watching a group of other people have a nice evening.

Have I played my non-alcoholic sympathy violin enough? Have I also given the impression that my friends are a group of alcoholics? I do sometimes wonder if we are too old for this behaviour to be normal. A bunch of lads in their twenties getting drunk is a sign of them having fun. A bunch of men in their forties getting drunk looks like a divorce-support group.

I spent around six months not drinking alcohol at all, and I have to say that I found there to be many more advantages than disadvantages. For one, I wouldn't have to worry that a casual meet-up with a friend would result in me not being able to work the next day. And the number of mysterious late-night breakages in our house was certainly reduced. It wasn't all fun, though, as I quickly discovered that non-alcoholic lager is very much the liquid equivalent of vegan cheese.

It's highly possible that you have read everything I've written above and are thinking that this doesn't reflect your experience with alcohol at all. You have spent your life drinking alcohol in moderation, being able to stop at exactly the right moment and keeping a steady buzz until you head to bed for a restful night's sleep and absolutely no hangover. Alcohol has simply been the lubricant in some of the best evenings of your life. I wish I was more like you. For me, alcohol has been the lubricant for some of the best middle sections of evenings, before I continue drinking and morph into a paralytic bell-end.

At the end of the six months, I faced a conundrum. Was I going to continue being teetotal or go back to drinking as before? I ended up choosing neither. I decided to conduct an experiment. If I could spend the next couple of months drinking, not solidly, but on evenings out, without making a cock of myself, then I would continue drinking. But if I woke up on any morning with a vague recollection of windmilling my chocolate acorn across the pub, then that would be my final sign to stop completely.

So far, so good. I have genuinely managed to keep my

drinking in moderation. On an evening out, I've even been known to recognize that I'm getting too battered and slow right down, perhaps even drinking a pint of water. This has, of course, led to the accusation that I am a lightweight, but I would rather that than risk waking up at home with a KFC bargain bucket next to the bed.

There are friends of mine who find it laughable if I suggest I have a problem with alcohol. There are people who drink to the point where they wake up in a ditch. I have done that on occasion, but not regularly. My issue is with the complete lack of control I have over how much I drink and how I behave. That could be anything from going to someone's house for a terrible after-party at 3 a.m. to simply expressing the view that sometimes I would rather listen to Harry Styles than Kendrick Lamar.

I guess the big problem with all of this is that whether you're being a dickhead or not is very much subjective. I could be in a situation where I'm out with my friends and I end up behaving like a complete twat. I then go home and go to bed. My friends set up a WhatsApp group, where they'll discuss what an annoying prick I've been that evening. What I've settled on is that I'll have a drink if I feel like it, but not always. It can be a little insulting to the person you are with, however, when they start to tell you how their home life is going and you say, 'Before you properly get into this story, I think I'm going to switch to tequila.'

Learning to Cook

There is no doubt that I should have done more cooking than I have at my age. When I was a kid I used to make omelettes, but it was only when I went to uni that I attempted actual cooking. I remember trying to make a pasta dish with tomato and melted mozzarella. To melt the mozzarella I threw it into a hot pan and stirred as it blackened into a substance that could only be removed by sandblasting. Then, rather than assuming I had done something wrong, I behaved as if this was some sort of anomaly, and took another pan and a second ball of cheese and ruined them both by exactly the same process. I didn't even phone my mum, whose recipe it was, to check the details with her. I simply did the same thing again and expected it for some reason to work the second time, the definition of madness.

When I moved in with Leesa, she announced that I was no longer allowed to cook on account of me taking two hours to make a stir-fry, and her deeming that fucking unacceptable. I couldn't tell you how I spent the time, save for the fact that I wanted it to be really good so I spent possibly the first hour googling hints and tips. What an hour of online research tells you about making a great stir-fry is that you definitely should have done this when you were at the shops buying stuff for a stir-fry, because now you are looking through a series of recipes that involve ingredients you don't have in the house. I was looking at a selection of meals I had no way of making, like some sort of Chinese cookery porn.

It would be very easy to blame this cookery ban for my failure to fire up the oven more often, but it's not like Leesa would stop me from stepping into the kitchen if I were determined. A healthy part of the reason is that I'm lazy. The other is that nobody else in the house likes the food I like – there's the obvious thing that I'm vegan, but the kids don't find that anywhere near as offensive as how spicy I like my food, Bacon Holy Fuck sauce and all. I would describe my children as spice averse – a crime, considering that by the time I was ten I was wolfing down dynamite curries like a stereotypical little Asian boy. My mum even once made me – and I can't quite believe this is real and not some sort of anxiety dream – a curry composed entirely of garlic. Imagine you had a lamb curry, except where you have lamb, this had garlic, and instead of potatoes there was garlic. I think there were some onions, to be fair. The next day I got on the school bus, secreting garlic through my skin, and everyone including friends started ripping me for smelling dreadful. It was the longest day of my life. One of the teachers spoke to me after a lesson to ask why I looked so upset. I had to explain that kids were being horrible to me because I smelt of garlic curry and all I could think was, 'This teacher must definitely have noticed how much I smell.'

Just the other day at dinner, my inaction in this area was

brought into sharp focus by the kids, who were joking around that I couldn't cook. This immediately pricked my ego, and I told them it wasn't that I couldn't, it was that I'm not allowed. In fairness to the children, they haven't seen much evidence of me even having basic common sense in the kitchen when I do step up. Just last night I was asked to put some dinner in the oven for the boys. When Leesa came home, she looked in the oven and asked me if I realized we had more than one child. Apparently I had not put in anywhere near enough chicken nuggets. I have no fucking idea how much nugget it takes to fill a child – I haven't even eaten chicken in thirty years. Leesa gathered the kids round and they all laughed so much at my incompetence that I half suspected Leesa had asked me to do the dinner as a joke. I was going to point out that I had been on a work call while I was doing it and so couldn't be blamed for the error, when it occurred to me that Leesa is often doing the dinner while on the phone and simultaneously regrouting the bathroom and she doesn't seem to make any mistakes.

I was put out, however, by the kids' assertion that I couldn't cook at all and I asked them to name a dish and said I would make it for them the very next day. Leesa immediately looked horrified, as she knew the kitchen would need to be replaced. I don't have the culinary skills to back up the boast but I was counting on the fact that I was talking to children and they had a limited range of dishes in their knowledge bank. I felt fairly confident they weren't going to request a salmon en croute. In fact, they asked for a chocolate cheesecake, which I know enough to know is an absolute piece of piss to make. I pretty much just needed to make sure to add enough sugar to the thing and I was golden – despite the fact that I was going to have to break the cardinal chef rule of tasting as you go, because that shit is just pure dairy.

I made and presented the cheesecake to the boys, and they were genuinely impressed. They said it was great and they took back their comments about me not being able to cook, and even said they would love it if I made it again. I was absolutely delighted right up until pretty much now, with my fingers on this keyboard, as it has just occurred to me that the boys have not requested it since. This might not sound like a big deal, but to put it into context, they requested Leesa made her vegan cupcakes again and they were fucking trash. I've now realized these pricks were humouring me.

My big issue at the moment is that I have still not learnt how to cook Sri Lankan food. This is an ongoing frustration for me. My mum is an incredible cook, and by rights I should be too, despite not having taken advantage of the fact my mum clearly wants to show me how to make these dishes as part of her legacy.

Everyone thinks their mum can cook, but, mate, my mum can cook – her Sri Lankan stuff absolutely bangs. I've tried loads of other versions of the dishes my mum makes and she does them the best. I know everyone says that but in my case it's true. She admitted to me recently that people often ask her for recipes and she tells them everything but leaves out a couple of spices from the ingredients so they can't get it quite the same. She said she would never do that to me, so I'm looking forward to testing how much she loves me. Although, to be fair, if my attempts taste different to hers I think I'll struggle to blame it on anything other than incompetence.

My mum drops off Asian care packages to keep me in curry. She does it quite often, and times it perfectly to the days when Leesa has done a fancy dinner. This has become such a bone of contention that when I did the show *Judge Romesh*, essentially me being Judge Judy, I was surprised to find that one of the cases was Leesa bringing my mum to court for messing up her meal plans. It was unbearable. I had no idea how much they were joking, and partway through the case I genuinely began to believe I was bringing the relationship between my mum and wife to an end for the purposes of the show. The worst turn was when Leesa revealed that she knew I'd been texting my mum to request the food, and I suddenly became the defendant. Everybody was finding it hilarious, while I was trying to glean from Leesa whether she was actually going to leave me. My mum even brought some curry to the show, which I felt was rubbing salty aubergine in the wounds, though to be fair I still ate it.

I don't know how I feel about learning how to cook my mum's curries. Although it would be a nice way to spend time with my mum, I don't know if I want to know how she makes them. I can't imagine telling her she doesn't need to bother making aubergine curry any more because I can do a passable job of it myself. I quite like the fact that if I want to eat those dishes, I have to contact her. I don't mean because I'm a lazy bastard, just that it's a nice experience for everyone involved. She feels great that her son needs her food, she brings it round, she sees her grandkids and we have a chat about what an amazing cook she is. Then she leaves our house feeling like the goddamned legend that she is. And then Leesa and I have an argument.

Trainer Geek

I have become obsessed with buying trainers. There are a number of reasons for this – it's a hip-hop thing, I'm trying to maintain some sort of grasp on my youth, and I have an addictive personality. This has resulted in a perfect storm.

There is a lot to unpack here in terms of ethics. I am a vegan, so I should not be buying trainers full stop. Very few pairs are vegan, and even fewer are made ethically. Now, you might be forgiven for owning one or two pairs of non-vegan child-labour trainers out of sheer necessity, but my desire to buy as many pairs as I can get my hands on is just plain offensive. I have become so obsessed, however, that if my own children could knock out a decent pair of Yeezys I'd consider putting them to it.

First, I have more shoes than I could ever possibly need. In a society where resources are scarce and not distributed equally, specifically meaning that some people don't have shoes at all, the decision to have as many as I have is at best naive and at worst capitalizing on my privilege. It's Western consumer culture at its worst. And having given myself a bit of a pass to consume these non-vegan items, I am consuming way more of them than I need to, which is like somebody saying they don't want to eat meat apart from chicken wings, then eating a thousand of them a day. And now I have to confess to only really writing this paragraph to make me feel better about continuing to buy trainers.

Let me be clear, I try to research and buy shoes that are made from richer canvas or synthetic leather, but you will always miss an upper or discover that the glue is made from the soul of a puppy or something.

Secondly, it is an utterly pointless waste of money. I've fallen victim to marketing. I'm buying limited-edition shoes that I've been informed are desirable and are therefore worth spending extra money on, despite there being nothing more impressive about the materials or design. I have got so far into trainers that my tastes have become extreme, and I end up buying retina-burning colours and patterns, and shoes moulded in the weirdest shapes. This is never more apparent than when I'm about to head out with the family and they all openly discuss how ugly my shoes are. I then get into a discussion about how they're actually really nice and the others don't know what they're talking about, while knowing deep down that I'm trying to deny the fact I've overpaid for something most people will think is hideous.

I think the ridiculousness of this hit me when I recently got incredibly excited about buying a pair of Air Jordan trainers because I'd had a pair when I was ten. I mean, what the fuck is going on? Am I going to extend this to all things I wore as a kid? Am I going to start rocking a Fraggles T-shirt again? Although, as I say that, I think I probably would and it would be great.

There is something very middle-aged bloke about collecting things. Men love finding something to waste their money on and become obsessive about, finding discussion forums and getting nerdy and sneering at people who don't know as much about their obscure passion as they do. That's very much the experience I have with hip-hop, except with trainers I don't know anywhere near enough and every now and again I ask some sort of question that gives away my lack of knowledge and I have to make an embarrassing climbdown. I'll ask a seller if they have green Jordan 6s and they'll say something like, 'Sure, just let me know which one of the seven green colour ways you're talking about, snarf,' and then I have to never contact them again.

I have now realized it's gone too far, and it wasn't the storage, it wasn't the money, and it wasn't the fact that the whole thing is absolutely tragic – it was the fact that I was out with Leesa and the kids, and I spent the whole time with my elbows poised to nudge them away if it looked like they were going to step on my shoes. If any of them do, I make enquiries about rehousing them. The kids, I mean.

Men have a weird relationship with clothing. Most men lock in on a signature outfit and wear that for ever, regardless of how age affects the look. For most British men, that signature outfit will almost always be bland as fuck. You often see a man wearing a polo shirt and you know he has worn variations of that outfit for the last twenty years. Men aren't necessarily at fault here – which is something you can't often say in 2020 – because men's clothing is generally fairly boring.

I get the convenience of going full Mark Zuckerberg on your outfit choices, and the only reason I've made any kind of effort with my dress sense is because I do television. There's no way I would otherwise have given anything approaching a shit about my appearance. Even when I'm getting dressed to do a TV show, I never think I'm going to look really good, my only objective is to not look awful. A few years ago I started doing *Mock The Week* regularly and I went through a phase of trying out different looks. It had been so long since I'd made any effort to dress well that I didn't even know what suited me. Those shows are now a record of failed outfit experiments, most of which I definitely shouldn't have tried. That shit is on the Dave channel for ever.

What's difficult for many men is that as we age, our bodies grow in a manner that is not conducive to making clothes look good. We hide under bigger and bigger sizes, our main concern being belly coverage, giving little thought to the aesthetic of the circus-tent silhouette we are creating. One of my biggest fears, as my body over-hangs my waistline precipice, is the slightly too short top that rises to reveal your belly every time you raise your arms. You go for a longer top to avoid that and to trick yourself that you look good, but it will widen across the belly and narrow beneath it, and when you see photos you realize you look a lot like a snake that's eaten a goat.

When men decide they are going to have a makeover or freshen up their look, they tend to throw money at labels and don't really give enough attention to how this stuff actually looks on them. This is in my own experience and

I have observed it in my friends as they increasingly fray around the edges too. My friendship group is littered with guys wearing Ralph Lauren tops that don't quite fit to the point where the horse looks a bit distorted. This isn't helped by the fact that men also tend to wear exactly the same jeans regardless of the rest of the outfit, and this is because most men choose trousers by smelling the crotch and deciding if they can get another day out of them. There is also the issue of torsos growing more quickly than hips and legs which means men increasingly look like a melting ice cream in a cone.

I'm writing this as if I'm operating on a different plane. I'm as guilty as anyone of being a shite dresser. I look in envy at Leesa as she rocks cool look after cool look. Is it too much for a man to ask that somebody compliment his outfit on an occasion when he isn't wearing an unusually smart suit? That is literally the only time men have their sartorial choices commended, and what might seem like a 'you look good' compliment is actually a way of saying, 'It hadn't occurred to me that you would have the skill set to look presentable based on the fact that you usually dress so tragically.'

I'm being a little bit self-defeating here. There are fantastically dressed men, of course – and they tend to be the ones who move in music and film circles and therefore are allowed to be a bit experimental with their looks, because either they are genetically gifted or else so popular that they could wear a bag of sausages and people would think they look fantastic. Regular blokes do not have that luxury. Try being a bloke and going to meet your friends wearing a slightly different cut of jeans – you will get destroyed. 'Oh, look who it is, Travolta's here, someone's been shopping in the women's section.' I know you are supposed to be fierce enough to not care about haters and just embrace your inner fabulousness, but the truth is that swagger just doesn't work in the Punch Bowl in Crawley.

It's been as adventurous as I can get to start wearing less baggy jeans and brighter colours, taking new garments on smaller evenings out to test the waters before becoming brave enough to wear them when more people might be about and ready to attack. And I have been targeted for roasting on many nights out. I have been accused of 'having a go', 'trying to be hot' and even 'having a midlife crisis', which forced me to return the satin jacket. This ongoing friendly fire has cowed me into finding myself a uniform and sticking to it, terrified of being seen to be making too much of an effort.

The lockdown pushed me, as many others, into a brand new area – snazzy loungewear. I have no idea why I haven't rocked this gear before. All this time I've been looking at teenagers wearing baggy tracksuits and thinking they look like a bunch of bell-ends, and now I've realized these roadmen are all dressing for comfort. It's been an incredible discovery – who the hell doesn't want to feel like they are spending the entire day in pyjamas?

The slight problem with this get-up is it doesn't look smart in the slightest. I would go as far as to say that while it looks borderline on younger guys, men of my age should not be seen wearing any of this at all. However, it is so damn comfortable that I am not willing to give it up just because I look ridiculous. So, for that reason, I'm now wearing it all the time, and arriving at places explaining that I was running late with the kids or something and unable to get changed into anything more suitable. It's the perfect solution – not only are you comfortable, but when everybody decides they want to head on to a late-night bar to carry on an evening that anyone with any kind of sense or sobriety would realize has run its course, you can point out that there is no way you are going to get in with tracky bottoms on. You can head home in the sort of comfort that can only be achieved with the perfect polyester cotton blend. And you're already ready for bed. For all my fretting about not dressing well enough and trying to be adventurous, I have pretty much regressed to dressing like a 13-year-old with incredibly high-end trainers. And I love it.

Music

Music is absolutely incredible, right? I mean, we all think that, don't we? At least, that's what I assumed until I met my wife. Leesa can go months without pressing *Play* on a song. I cannot believe it. She has songs she likes, and she does enjoy hearing them, but she would not go out of her way to put one on, and has no desire to hear more music or stay across any new releases.

That last one is partly an age thing. If you're like me, you'll have been through a phase of aggressively consuming anything that comes out, learning every lyric and all the liner notes, and essentially internalizing each record. Then, most people get to a point where they decide they're pretty much done with staying across new music and they cycle through what they know and like over and over again, occasionally listening to something new by accident and only if it happens to sound a lot like something they already listen to.

I don't think there's anything wrong with that — I think the pleasure we can still get from hearing a song for the thousandth time is one of the things that makes music so incredible. When I was about six years old, I remember

watching TV while having breakfast and they were playing the video of 'I Just Called To Say I Love You' by Stevie
Wonder, arguably one of his worst songs but undeniably
catchy. I was particularly excited for school that day, possibly because I had extra sandwiches. Even now, every
time I hear that song, I feel exactly like I did then – the
feeling comes back to me vividly. I love music for the same
reason I love comedy and horror movies – it elicits a vis-
ceral reaction and makes you involuntarily feel a certain
way, and I am fully in favour of achieving that without
having to resort to medication.

I particularly enjoy it when music makes you feel miserable. I don't mean being reminded of genuine tragedy,
but you know when you got dumped ages ago? And then
you sat and listened to R'n'B and cried a lot? No? Just
me? OK, well, one of my favourite things is to put those
songs on and feel sad again. Is that weird? You listen to
those songs, feel upset about getting dumped when you
were a teenager, then you look at your wife and your
brain connects that upset with her and you end up having some sort of argument. That's how I like to enjoy
music.

Although I don't listen to music as much as I used to, I
am partial to walking to the shops with a song on that I
pretend is the soundtrack to the film I'm in. One of my
favourites is 'Fuck You' by Pharoahe Monch. It's one of
those songs that's just about being a badass, and I imagine
everybody is hearing it as they watch me walk around the
Co-op selecting tortilla chips.

Many times I've been convinced that life would be

better if people could hear certain music when they saw you. I envision a future when we are all fitted with in-ear speakers that are open to Bluetooth connections. You could turn up to a night out with your mates and transmit entrance music to them. Or if you were going to meet someone for lunch and were feeling a bit down, you could play a sad song as you walk in. I mean, as I describe it now it feels pretty invasive and there is probably no way this is a good idea, but my point is I really think life would be better if we all had our own soundtracks.

Part of the reason I don't listen to as much music as I used to is that I'm banned from listening to hip-hop in the house unless I can find a selection of family-friendly radio edits. I was so determined to make this work that I put together a Spotify playlist made exclusively of hip-hop songs that had the swearing bleeped out. Then Leesa realized that radio edits are no good. Surprisingly enough, when our children hear the sound f —— ck, they actually manage to work out what the word is supposed to be. For that reason, in order to be permitted to listen to rap music in the house, I have to find songs that didn't have swearing in in the first place, which basically means I can't listen to anything released after 1991.

I had always assumed that because I'm so obsessed with music, my kids were going to think that what I listened to was really cool. I now find myself in a position where my children say the same sort of things to me as my parents used to say when I was a kid:

'It doesn't sound like music.'

'It's just a lot of shouting and swearing.'

My kids are such fucking squares.

Our kids listen to the same kind of pop shit all children listen to. And of course I have no issue with that. However, I know for a fact that I first fell in love with Public Enemy's album *It Takes A Nation Of Millions To Hold Us Back* when I was eleven years old. Our eldest son is about to turn eleven, which means I am about to start judging him. I'm really excited. The next few years of his music-listening career are going to shape his life so much. Discovering hip-hop when I did had such an impact on me that one of my favourite parts of my job now I'm in my forties is the hip-hop podcast. That very much sounds like me trying to plug the podcast in this book, but my point is the music he is about to get into will likely stay with him for life. I don't mind what he chooses, but given it's likely to be blaring out of his teenage bedroom soon I'm in the middle of a covert operation to steer him away from Justin Bieber. Although I would say that 'Sorry' is an absolute banger.

Sometimes in the car, when we have my music on, my wife will look at me in disbelief, as if to question that a grown man who is also a father of three would choose to listen to that sort of thing. I always respond by telling her that this is a particular type of hip-hop I'm not terribly keen on, and actually the stuff I prefer is a lot more grown-up and less aggressive. That is a lie. There is nothing I enjoy more than hammering the Volvo down to the dump while listening to convoluted stories about a drug deal that turned into a gun fight before they headed home to finish the evening with a cheeseburger and some sort of orgy. I really love the immature badman stuff. I obviously like the more mature, well-rounded artists too, but there is a place for all of it in my record collection. I just have to pretend to be appalled by some lyrics for my wife's benefit, and hope she doesn't blame me when the kids start swearing.

Get a Tattoo (If You Want)

I got my first tattoo after our first child was born. I decided to get his name on my shoulder. Leesa said she was going to do the same but she bottled it – a betrayal I haven't yet forgiven her for. In fact, I am considering getting one that says 'Leesa really let me down'. After that, I added our second son's name, but to this day I haven't managed to get around to having our youngest one's done. He hasn't noticed yet, but I suppose I'm going to have to do it at some point because I really don't want that to be something he explains to a counsellor.

This was enough to trigger something of an addiction. The next tattoo I got was a portrait of Richard Pryor on my forearm. I love Richard Pryor, and the image on my arm is based on my favourite photo of him. I love that tattoo and stand by it, but my friends have never understood why I had it done. I remember Seann Walsh taking one look at it and pissing himself laughing. We had a conversation about whether you would have any British comedian on your arm. He is another hero, but it would somehow seem weird to have Jack Dee inked on your body. Plus the next time I saw Jack I'm pretty sure he would think I'm a lunatic.

Many people say they would never get a tattoo because

they worry they would come to regret it. I cannot relate to that in the slightest. At the worst you are going to have a funny story to tell. The idea that I must only adorn my body with timeless pieces of art or else preserve my virgin skin would be to give my physical appearance a little too much credit. People say, 'Imagine what that will look like when you're seventy.' I can't imagine that anyone in the retirement home is going to look at me and say, 'He is so fucking hot, if only he didn't have that Autobot tattoo on his leg.'

Leesa doesn't seem to give a shit, to the point where I don't even tell her I'm having them done. I'm sure if I returned home with a face tattoo she would be concerned, but otherwise I think I'm pretty much free to do whatever I like, though she'd probably prefer I didn't get a new tattoo immediately before a family holiday that involves water-parks. But despite my wife's nonchalance, other people seem to hold very strong opinions about what I do with my own body. I'm sure this is true for anyone with tattoos and piercings, but it has always baffled me.

I genuinely did get an Autobot tattoo on my calf because I love Transformers and I am a man-child. The Michael Bay movies made me slightly question that decision because he really did shit all over that whole world for me. Those films are so awful that I briefly contemplated laser removal, but ultimately I stand by the tattoo partly because I really do love Transformers and partly because the laser treatment is painful. Optimus Prime would have to be unmasked as a sex offender for me to really consider it.

I was out with friends when the conversation moved on to the subject of Transformers, which admittedly makes my friends and me sound like an absolute bunch of losers, but hold on. We were in fact reminiscing about a lads' holiday to Faliraki, where I was having a heated discussion with a friend about who would win in a fight between Galvatron and Megatron, and my friend completely lost his shit and started screaming at me about how I always think I'm better than everyone and I should watch myself. Now, *that* is the story that confirms my friends and I are an absolute bunch of losers.

After our brief Faliraki throwback, I then revealed that I had earlier that week got an Autobot tattoo, at which point everyone entered into a discussion about how sad they thought it was. There was nobody on my side at all. With the understanding that of course it was sad, it became a discussion about exactly how sad it was. As sad as men who take their tops off when it's sunny? Maybe even as sad as people who post pictures of British soldiers on Facebook because they're annoyed there's halal meat at Subway? I argued my case, but it proved that people really do feel strongly about the permanence of a tattoo and the decision behind it, even if it's not on their body.

When we were filming series 1 of *The Ranganation*, one of the members of the panel, known as Metalhead, revealed that he'd had a tattoo of me done on his leg. I didn't believe it at first, but was incredibly touched when he showed it to me. It made me think that I shouldn't become a sex pest or end up in prison or do anything that would damage my reputation and cause him to regret that tattoo. I would hate to think that he might start telling people it was Rolf Harris to avoid embarrassment.

On the last episode of the show, we were going to discuss tattoos and I mentioned that it would be funny to get Metalhead tatted on to my leg. The production team thought it would be funny too but said obviously it couldn't be a real one. I said I thought it wasn't worth doing if it wasn't a real tattoo. They agreed, but said they couldn't be seen to be encouraging me to do it. I then had to sign something saying that neither they nor the BBC were encouraging or forcing me to get a tattoo. This all felt mad to me because I have now become dangerously casual about what I have written and drawn on my body. I would go so far as to say that if everyone clubbed together a healthy donation for a good charity I would happily get a penis tattooed on my back, or, worse still, the Spurs cockerel. (Please don't take that as a suggestion.)

After signing the forms I went down to the tattoo place, where one of the production team also had to film me saying I was there of my own accord and wasn't being coerced into it in any way. I got the tattoo done and did the big reveal on the final episode of the show. I now have Metalhead on my leg, and it genuinely made for about forty seconds of TV. There is a strong argument there that it wasn't worth it. But Metalhead is a top bloke, and I'm happy and it's given me something to put in this book. Look out in the future for a book called *Romesh's Tattoo Stories* with me completely covered in ink on the cover, because I have run out of other shit to talk about.

Now, I'm fully aware that some people get tattoos they later regret and spend a lot of money getting them removed. If like me, however, you're generally happy to treat your skin like a teenager's pencil case, then I say go for it. Why not get that unicorn on your arse, or Jeremy Corbyn on your thigh? It's your body, do what you want. What I would say is this: I am absolutely not the person you should be coming to for tattoo advice.

Eat the Doughnuts

Veganism has become a whole lot easier recently. When I first changed my diet a few years ago, you had to accept that desserts weren't happening for you, and that the only sweet treat you might be offered is a vegan cake that somebody made at their house using pickle brine instead of egg and you would have to pretend that it tasted like a regular cake or you would seem ungrateful. Most desserts involve some sort of dairy or egg, and so, in the past, you would almost always be offered fruit, rather than the cakes or ice cream everybody else was tucking into.

Now we are at a stage where vegan desserts and cakes have progressed massively, which I would argue makes it incredibly difficult to stay healthy. More vegan treats are available than ever, and they taste delicious, but they still require a bit of effort to get hold of. This is an extremely tricky place to be for a greedy vegan. Let me paint the picture for you.

Last year I was in a writing room for a sitcom I was working on. This is essentially where a group of people throw around as many funny ideas as they can while also trying not to eat too much. It's a tough pair of objectives. One morning, Yasmine Akram walked in with a box of the most incredible doughnuts I had ever seen. What a lovely thing to do – a complete mood booster. She went on to say that she didn't want me to feel left out and so had bought a selection of vegan doughnuts as well. This was incredibly thoughtful, but it put me in a position where, to my mind, I had to eat every single one of those doughnuts. Nobody else was going to touch them because they were vegan, and they wouldn't want to take them from the guy with the dietary disability. On top of that, they'd be convinced they're not as nice as the regular ones and wouldn't want them anyway. Similarly, Yasmine had gone to all that trouble and I didn't want to offend her. So I ate every one of the five doughnuts. They were, to be fair, very moreish, but imagine if I had turned to Yasmine and told her I was trying to watch what I ate. She would have been so gutted. I had to eat them. It was my duty as a friend and colleague.

Later on that day I had to record the last few pieces of voiceover for another show. As I sat down to chat to the director in the edit suite, a couple of guys from the production company came in and said, 'Romesh, we wanted to celebrate getting the show wrapped, so we got you some vegan doughnuts from this amazing new place,' and opened a box of exactly the same doughnuts I had just eaten so many of. I obviously didn't tell them this. I ate the doughnuts, tried not to throw up during the voiceover, then headed home to call the NHS helpline to tell them about my afternoon of giving myself type-2 diabetes.

As sob stories go, I'm aware this isn't a great one. 'Oh my God, it's so tough for me! People keep going out of their way to buy me lovely vegan doughnuts and I have to eat them to avoid offending anyone – why doesn't anyone appreciate what I'm going through?!' I get it – it's a bit 'Sam Smith sitting outside their mansion and crying during lockdown'.

The point I'm trying to make is that having your veganism specially catered for makes it almost impossible not to eat everything put in front of you. And because vegan doughnuts and cakes are still a novelty, I'm under intense pressure to try them all. Every single time a new vegan wonder product comes out I think, 'Here we go, I'm going to have to get that.' And then I do, and I buy more of them because I'm worried that they won't sell enough to become a permanent product, and then I'm out of an evening and somebody approaches me to ask me how I manage to be so fat as a vegan. It's a tough life.

Doughnuts: I really can't understand why some people don't like them. It's a bread cake covered in icing and shaped like a ring. How the hell can you not like that? Sometimes they are filled with even more deliciousness – are people seriously saying they don't like these things? Leesa says she doesn't. If ever I have brought doughnuts home she has looked at them and said something like, 'I don't know how you eat them, they are so sweet.' Whereas, I see them as little nuggets of joy in a world that is otherwise bleak and awful.

Leesa is my wife and so I have made allowances, since there is a body of evidence to suggest that, despite not being into doughnuts, she is a decent person. I do think, however, that if somebody doesn't like doughnuts for a reason that isn't health- or lifestyle-related, it suggests something deeply wrong with them that I can't get on board with.

I watched a Jeff Garlin stand-up special where he talked about spending the day on set eating doughnuts and by the time he got to the end of shooting he realized he had eaten thirty of them. I totally relate to that. To you, that might read like a man who is out of control and something needs to be done, and indeed Jeff took action to overhaul his diet, but to me there is another side to that story: where a man has the superpower of being able to enjoy his thirtieth doughnut as much as he enjoys his first. In a life where things are so challenging and difficult, why wouldn't you eat so much delicious sugar and dough that you yourself become a doughnut?

I have only in this last couple of years realized that it is probably a good idea to keep track of what I eat. As I've said, in the past I always assumed that the body wants what the body wants, and if that happens to be thirty-nine poppadoms, then so be it. I thought everybody was like that. Then I discovered that most people I know actually have a much better grip on their food intake than I do.

Greed is something I have had to accept I need to deal with. I think about food constantly. People will be talking about work and I'm thinking: 'How can anybody be focused on this when there are no snacks in the room?' If I make something at home, my instinct is to cook all of the ingredients available and then eat the whole thing, regardless of the size. If Linda McCartney sausage rolls came in boxes of forty-eight I would be doing batch bakes of those and then smashing them down with seven cans of Diet Coke.

That's my other issue – Diet Coke. I am addicted to the stuff. It has zero calories and so I have swapped water for it. There is no way that that can be OK. Diet Coke has a list of ingredients that sound like what you'd use to cook meth. It took an external trigger to make me consider cutting down. We were watching *The Stranger* on Netflix and one of the characters talked about trying to give up Diet Coke. I was hit by the realization that no matter how many cans of Diet Coke the writers had imagined that character drinking, I drank more. While my wife continued watching the show, I descended into a phone vortex of online research into what this stuff was doing to my body.

I sometimes wonder if Leesa can believe what's going on. We sit down to watch a show together and everything seems fine. Then the programme finishes and she looks across to find me in the middle of a silent panic attack because I've spent the last half hour googling 'Will Diet Coke kill Romesh Ranganathan?' I decided, after that ruined evening of quality time, that I would limit myself to one can a day, which is still more than most people on the planet consume but signifies a huge reduction for me.

That daily can is an ordeal. Every sip is me worrying it will be the last. I finish it and spend the rest of the day wishing I hadn't drunk it when I did. I start planning when I'm going to have tomorrow's can. Maybe I should put one in the fridge tonight so it's at optimum temperature for the next day? Maybe I should just wake up and have it for breakfast? Effectively I am thinking about Diet Coke far more than I was before I imposed this restriction on it. I think it's fair to say this is evidence that I have a serious problem and should probably give it up completely. Also, there is absolutely no way I'm a good advert for Diet Coke. I imagine I could get some sort of reverse sponsorship deal, where they pay me to dissociate myself from their product.

It has occurred to me that it's probably a good idea to limit yourself on everything. I think putting in restraints and tests of willpower is good for the soul. It introduces a bit of discipline, and that's worthwhile. It is for that reason that I started intermittent fasting. And you already know how that went.

Uncoordinated

As I write these very words, my face is contorting in pain. This is my first writing session with a newly broken left wrist and a dislocated right thumb. I am so bloody embarrassed. We were doing a BMX challenge for *A League Of Their Own* – me, Freddie Flintoff, Jamie Redknapp and Rob Beckett. Now, these things get thoroughly assessed beforehand. Many of the production team had gone round the track to test it and it had been deemed safe.

The warning bells should have rung for me when I couldn't make it all the way round the kids' track we were starting out on. What I hadn't appreciated was that going up the bumps required you to acquire enough speed on the downhill bits. What this meant was the three of them would go round with no trouble at all, while I would make it to the second bump and have to get off the bike. What made it even bleaker was that normally the lads have a big old laugh at how shit I am at stuff, but on this occasion it looked so pathetic they actually started giving me tips. It was awful.

I carried this fear of humiliation into our practice on the main track. We were each asked to tackle the sticky part of the track and would then get feedback from the instructors. Nervously I went for it, and I made my way round with no problems. I was starting to think I was going to be OK. By 'be OK' I mean I would get round the course without making a twat of myself and then everyone would cheer and encourage me like you do the kid who comes last in everything on sports day. Which actually was also me. The next stage was for us to race each other in pairs. It was me and Jamie up first. We took the first turn and went over the first set of bumps and I actually got through ahead of Jamie. That was amazing. After an ugly duckling start in training, was I going to show myself to have actual talent in something physical?

The answer was provided instantly as I went over a bump too quickly (for me – in reality I was riding at barely a canter), hit the next bump hard and then swatted head-first straight into the ground, genuinely feeling like I'd shattered every bone in the top half of my body, although to be fair I am a massive baby.

Medical staff rushed in to treat me, and I was appalled to see my thumb looking like it was trying to escape from my hand. I imagined they were going to have to shove that straight back in and it would be really painful and I would cry and never live it down, so I started to freak out a bit. The embarrassment gods must have taken pity on me, though, because the thumb just kind of popped back in itself.

The embarrassment was not over, however. I had to walk away with an ice pack suspended from each hand, leading Freddie's son to comment I looked like a T-Rex. It was a weird one at the hospital because I was convinced that I had absolutely shagged both hands, so when they told me it was just a broken wrist and a thumb injury I was relieved, despite the fact that a both-hands injury can't help but look a bit embarrassing. My biggest fear was having to tell Leesa she was going to have to wipe my arse. When I found out that wouldn't be necessary I contemplated telling her she had to and letting her believe it for a day for shits and giggles. I realized it might end up being more 'shits and Leesa leaving me' so in the end I decided against it.

Lots of people in the show felt guilty and kept apologizing, but I just felt so mortified. Because this had been declared safe as houses. People had tested it numerous times and it had been fine. The experts saw no potential issues, so we can only surmise that my levels of incompetence and lack of coordination were beyond their testing boundaries. They were simply not anticipating someone being as fucking useless as me.

A League Of Their Own is a show that has seen me through some courage breakthroughs, and has meant that I'm now willing to do much more than I used to. I remember first appearing on the show a few years ago. When you arrive at the studio they ask you to go and have a look at the end-of-show challenge to familiarize yourself with what's required and become as accustomed as you can to the shit-scariness of it.

On that show, I had to ride a bike on a treadmill. The treadmill would then be lifted to the roof of the studio and I would be tilted backwards, and I would have to ride it for as long as I could. This sounded awful, made even more awful by the fact I couldn't even ride the fucking thing when the treadmill was on the ground. It was almost amusing to see the producers tell me it was absolutely fine and to just take my time, while in reality I could tell they needed me to master it as soon as possible.

I was so shit scared of doing that challenge that I don't remember being able to say anything else during the show. I just remember sitting in the seat for the entirety of the time thinking, 'You're going to die at the end of this show, how can you be funny? You literally have hours of your life left.'

I've done countless challenges since then. People often ask me if I'm putting on an act of being terrified of every single challenge, but I'm not in the slightest. For me, there are two clear fears at play here – one is the fear of the challenge itself, and the other is the fear of being so remarkably and consistently shit at every single one of them. Every week the producers talk about how amazing it would be if I was able to beat everyone, and every week I let them down by being predictably awful. The only time I've ever done anything good was on a powerboat challenge when victory did not depend upon my physical prowess.

The reason I mention all this is I have managed to engineer a situation where my job requires me to essentially be the shittest kid in PE, except I'm an adult and there's usually a camera in my face. It was bad enough in school, when the other kids didn't want to be on the same team as you, or when the teacher would give you a head start, not for any kind of disability, but just because you were so blisteringly shit at everything. I was even shitter than the other shit kids.

There are people who have fond memories of sports and PE in school, who did great, and probably continue to play sport now because they enjoy it and it gives them a buzz. And they probably look at adults who don't exercise and say things like, 'I just don't understand why some people don't engage in competitive sports!' Maybe when you don't get picked and you lose every time and you're breathing out your arse, it doesn't quite have the same appeal, mate.

But then what happens is you leave school and you're able to put that behind you. You can exercise in a gym if you want to or go running and you never again have to make a dick of yourself in front of people who are much better than you. I, on the other hand, have chosen to relive that exact experience as my livelihood.

In fairness to Freddie and Jamie, they are never nasty about what to them must seem a magical lack of ability to do anything requiring coordination or physical exertion. They must observe me with the same sort of bemused intrigue we do when we see a monkey trying to solve a puzzle on a science documentary, the difference being that the monkey eventually cracks it.

I am convinced that the stereotype that footballers are thick has been promoted by a selection of people who were shit at sports at school and so want to see physical abilities ridiculed or perceived as less valuable than intellect. It's a snobbery that goes both ways, as the sporties stereotype those less gifted as boring no-sex-having losers. Though I can attest to some of that definitely being true.

To be honest, those previous paragraphs are not quite the pioneering insight I hoped they would be, but I do genuinely believe that your physical abilities as a child have huge ramifications on your life experiences, not just in sport but socially, at least for blokes.

If you are good at sports or even into sports, you tend to be more alpha, which tends to mean more popular, which means better with girls, which means you build more confidence as you grow older, which tends to mean you have confidence in other aspects of life, which possibly means you're better in job interviews and haggling and dealing with confrontation and all those other traditionally masculine things.

There is also the issue of attractiveness. We can talk as much as we like about beauty only being skin deep but Freddie and Jamie are much better looking than me, and their physiques are to die for.

Whenever I say anything like this, somebody will say, 'Don't be silly, I find you attractive because of who you are, you're making that up.' Am I? On the last series of *League*, we did a marines training weekend. Jamie posted a photo of the three of us in uniform. There were, no exaggeration, hundreds of comments about how fit Jamie and Freddie were and how people would love to jump their bones or take them round the barracks, or invade their borders, or whatever military imagery they could come up with for shagging them unconscious.

A few hundred comments down the list, there was one lone response that mentioned me. A woman posted, 'I love men in uniform. They are so hot that even Romesh looks all right.'

The one great thing about having no coordination is

that it's a shortcoming I can't do anything about. I can't practise my way to not being physically deficient. There's some kind of liberation in the fact that although I am fucking useless, at least it's something that's out of my control, like my limbs appear to be. I just have to accept that if I am at the park and someone throws me a frisbee, or I'm on holiday and someone pulls out a beach bat and ball set, or even if someone just kicks a ball to me in the park, I am moments away from humiliation. I pray my kids are not cursed in the same way.

Movies

It has taken me my whole life, but I have now accepted that, despite my love for films, my taste in them is genuinely appalling. A while ago, a friend asked if I wanted to curate an evening at his film festival. He asked me to send him my selections, which I did, and he replied telling me that I had the movie taste of a teenager, and also that it was probably best I didn't do the festival. The saddest thing about this episode is that I had deliberately chosen the more sophisticated films from my list.

I don't know if this is particular to comedians, or just middle-class people, which most comedians are, but whenever I talk about films with any of them, they are able to describe the work of directors at a level that means I am completely lost within about a minute and a half of the conversation starting. However, my ego means I cannot admit I'm out of my depth and instead I spend the rest of the chat nodding and saying things like, 'Absolutely. Couldn't agree more.'

I recently guested on an episode of Brett Goldstein's brilliant movie podcast, where he asked me what I thought was objectively the best film ever made. I said,

Eternal Sunshine Of The Spotless Mind. I don't even think that's true. I loved that film, don't get me wrong, but there is absolutely no fucking way that that is objectively the best film ever made. As soon as I said the words, I could see Brett's face try not to betray the fact that I was probably a mistake booking and that it was in his best interests to pretend he'd forgotten to record our chat. He then listened as I tried to justify my answer, and somehow managed to keep a straight face as even I lost faith in what I was saying mid-sentence. At some point I'm sure Brett started to wonder if I'd even understood the question.

I have opinions that mean I cannot be reasonably included in any discussion about movies. For example, I believe that the Back to the Future trilogy is the best trilogy ever made. I realize that three was a little bit weaker than the other two; I realize that there are a number of time-travel story loopholes that require you to suspend disbelief before you can enjoy the films, but I also think that any day where you sit down to watch those films back-to-back is a great one. I mean, obviously, if you are watching those films to distract you from a violent bout of gastro-enteritis, then you're probably not having the best time, but I would still argue that it's a good day.

A lot of you would put forward a more artsy trilogy for consideration, like perhaps the Godfather movies, ignoring the fact that Godfather Part III is more of an abomination than seeing Doc Brown riding a time-travel train. Others of you might argue that no one in their right mind would look

179

beyond the original Star Wars trilogy. But I'm done with Star Wars. There have been more shit Star Wars films than good ones, and they have absolutely milked that teat dry, blue milk and all.

It's a weird one when you watch those films through children's eyes. I took my eldest son to watch *The Force Awakens* at the cinema, which is essentially a remake of the first Star Wars movie. My son absolutely loved it, and asked about watching the originals. I didn't want to say no, but I knew he'd be disappointed. The first Star Wars film was made for a generation of people with a much longer attention span than he has. If you watch *The Force Awakens*, it cuts from scene to scene, from visual to visual, and never lets up in pace. There is no way my son has the patience to sit and watch Luke Skywalker basically have a cup of tea in Obi-Wan Kenobi's living room.

A recent set of films I have been obsessed with is the Avengers saga. I know Martin Scorsese described these films as lacking invention or surprise and many people are quite snobby about them, but I think they're absolutely incredible. When I went to watch *Iron Man* at the cinema with Leesa, I had no idea it would kick off such an amazing film journey. If you think about every superhero film or series, they all start with an origin story, then each subsequent film brings out a different baddie for the protagonist to take on. The Marvel films stick to that formula but they are brilliant at disguising it. They bring different heroes together, they raise the stakes to intergalactic level without it feeling too ridiculous, and they're even willing to kill off your favourites.

I did stand-up about the Avengers movies, and some-body in the audience complained about spoilers. Fuck off, mate. I'm sorry, you can't do spoiler warnings for ever. If the film is over a year old and you're not committed enough to have seen it, it's not my job to protect you. In that guy's defence, however, the films are coming out so quickly that staying across them actually starts to feel quite difficult.

One thing these films have to contend with is the fact that stuff that looks so good in comic books and cartoons looks absolutely ridiculous in real life. I would argue that the films that manage to cope with this successfully have won 90 per cent of the battle. For instance, the Batman films by Christopher Nolan were brilliant because they made the batshit concept of a man dressed as a bat striking fear into the hearts of criminals feel vaguely plausible. Let's put Batman's elitist politics to one side for this argu-ment. Then watch *Batman versus Superman* with Ben Affleck and Henry Cavill. That film looks fucking bananas. Ben Affleck looks like a man playing dress-up and the film genuinely ends with them making up because they realize their mums have got the same name. It's that kind of moment that reminds me I am an adult watching a film that is essentially a fancy-dress party.

I took my eldest son to watch *Avengers: Endgame*, a film that brought to a close a major storyline in the Marvel uni-verse. I have never seen a film that so blatantly required the viewer to know absolutely everything about all the films that came before it. It was almost arrogant. It was saying to the audience, 'If you haven't bothered to pay attention to all the previous films, you don't deserve to

understand this.' I spent most of the film trying to understand all the references and figure out what all the callbacks
were. I found it fairly stressful. Midway through the film,
I looked across at my son, who was watching in complete
and utter ecstasy. I immediately became paranoid. How
the shit was this kid following all this so much more effectively than me! I spent the latter part of the film desperately
trying to defuse my latest worry that I have some form of
dementia.

Worrying about having dementia has led me to down-
load Rosetta Stone Spanish, buy a Rubik's cube, do Sudoku,
and start playing weird mental games like thinking of
series of names that begin with every letter of the alpha-
bet. The trigger can be anything. Once it was because I
couldn't think of the word 'education' during a conversation about education. Another time it was when I couldn't
beat any of the children at the game Dobble. That sent me
into an absolute downward spiral. I started googling things
like, 'Are children particularly good at Dobble?' And
'Does me being bad at Dobble mean I could be put in a
home?' I overcame that particular period of worry by
downloading a mental arithmetic game on to my phone.

We left the cinema, and I was determined to find out
how my son had managed to process the film so much
better than I had. Obviously, it turns out he hadn't. He
hasn't even seen all the Marvel films. The difference
between my son and me is that he realized you can just
enjoy the film for what it is: stuff blowing up in an entertaining way. There is no need to understand every single
nuance and clue and Easter egg. I once again realized I was

being an idiot and went home to do level-three Spanish on my laptop.

I am fortunate to have a group of friends who are as thick as me. What this means is I can happily enter into discussions with them about how the villain in *Black Panther* is possibly the best bad guy in the history of cinema and none of them take the piss out of me for being a lowbrow twat. When you are in polite company, however, for example when meeting the other halves of your wife's new group of friends, it can be embarrassing when the talk turns to films and you pontificate on how unnecessary it was for Christopher Nolan to show us the shot of Alfred at the end of *The Dark Knight Rises*, and then you realize they want to discuss world cinema and the purple patch that Norwegian arthouse is going through.

I have had a recent breakthrough, however. I love the film-review podcast by Mark Kermode and Simon Mayo. I listen to it religiously. A while back, Mark Kermode was reviewing the film *Parasite*. He described it as being brilliant Korean cinema, and you shouldn't allow the subtitles to stop you enjoying this masterpiece. Well, I was very cynical. This sounded like exactly the sort of thing that Leesa's new friends' husbands would be discussing.

It was on the plane on the way to a holiday that I saw the film was available for in-flight viewing. I decided to give it a spin. I was surprised to discover that I absolutely loved it. It's simply brilliant. It's one of the best films I've ever seen, subtitles or not, and almost certainly would be a better answer to the question, 'What is, objectively, the best film ever made?' I didn't even enjoy it in a wanky 'this is the sort of thing I should be enjoying' way. I just enjoyed it in the same way that I like *Iron Man 3*. I walked off that plane feeling like an intellectual colossus. I'm thinking about holding my own film festival. I'll just show *Parasite* and the Back to the Future trilogy.

Builders

My name is Romesh Ranganathan and builders terrify me. I'm so averse to the whole idea of having any kind of building work done at our house that I usually leave it until we're suffocating under the weight of a collapsed wall before I decide to call them in. I'm nervous about expressing my views on builders and home improvers because I don't want to be blacklisted and have to deal with some sort of tradesmen vendetta for the rest of my life, but the truth is, if you told me that had already happened, I would believe you. I think I radiate some sort of energy that builders can detect, where they know they can overcharge and underdeliver and there will be absolutely no comeback. I don't know what I find more difficult to deal with – the fact I can never quite get what I want from them, or the fact I turn into my best appropriation of a silverback whenever I'm around them.

I'm not sure what it is that makes me change my behaviour, but it might be because, despite the fact it's 2020 and gender roles are an archaic relic, I'm emasculated by having men in the house who are so much better than me at something traditionally manly. Then I have to show them through the house and they'll notice that all our dining room chairs are wonky and say, 'Bloody hell, mate, were you pissed when you did those?' and I tell them my wife put them together, even though it was me, and she told me I was doing it wrong at the time, and every time somebody comes and comments on them it is a reminder of my failings as a man.

A few years ago, I wanted to convert the garage into an office. This is because I find it very difficult to work in the house because of the noise, and Leesa finds it very difficult to not interrupt me. Part of the problem is what I do for a living is so unimportant as a thing that people, even Leesa, can't believe I take it seriously. I will be at my laptop doing some work and she will say something that needs to be said urgently, like, 'Bloody hell, you should have seen what Sarah was wearing on the school run today', and I will say, 'Yeah, I just kind of need to get on with this', and she will reply, 'Yes, of course, you need to be able to concentrate on your jokes about calling everyone a prick.' And so it was by mutual agreement that I started to work in the garage, which is where I'm writing this now. As I look around, I see I'm surrounded by all my music, comic books and comedy memorabilia, and it has just occurred to me that I'm actually being moved out of the house.

I digress. We needed a builder to convert the garage and I wanted to make sure I didn't mess up by choosing the wrong person to do it. I'd already had the experience of asking someone to fit a shower and they managed to fix it in place so that whenever you turned it on, it pissed water into the brickwork. We only found out when our neighbours called us round to show us the water seeping through their side of the wall. What I find amazing is that part of building training appears to be how to react to every situation as if you've never encountered it before. 'What's that? Shower in the bathroom? Well, that's a tricky one, to be honest. The problem is that installing a shower after a bathroom has been fitted means you're upsetting the bathroom balance, which could lead to some settlement issues. The bathroom kind of reacts against the change and that can negatively affect the shower fitting, which is why it's leaking water into the wall. I did warn you this could happen.' By the end of it I was apologizing to this prick for having the type of wall that encourages leaking.

What makes this worse is that my brother is so much better at any sort of improvement work than I am. If it's a small job, he will watch a YouTube video and then do it himself. Just last month he did his bathroom tiling. He posted the picture on Facebook and everybody talked about what a great job he'd done, praising his manly self-sufficiency. I once looked up on YouTube how to fit a new bathroom light fixture and I managed to both break the fitting and electrocute myself, which meant that Leesa had to pretend to feel sorry for me while also pissing in the dark for two months.

In order to avoid problems, I decided to go on one of those websites where all the builders have previous recommendations, because there is absolutely no way that those could be faked by the builders themselves. You have to put in the job requirements, and it comes back with a list of builders who are up to the job and will come and give you a quote for it. This is the first issue. I know you're supposed to get a number of people round and have them assess the job, get quotes and then have a family meeting where you decide who you are going to get to do the work.

What happens with me is that I invite the first person round and I'm so desperate to get a move on with it that if they don't look like a serial killer and quote me a million pounds, then I'll use them. I realize this is part of the reason I've had some bad experiences, but I still haven't deviated from a policy that means all the builders I've used have names beginning with A.

The other issue is choice. There's way too much of it. When I filled in the details on the website, I listed the job as 'Convert garage to office'. As far as I'm concerned, that's all the detail required. Make it happen. Turn my garage into an office like magic and I will walk in when it's done and go 'Ooh wow' like the end of *60 Minute Makeover*. That's not what happens, though. What happens is the builder turns up and asks you how you actually want it done. I don't fucking know. He said to me, 'What type of office are you looking for?' and I genuinely answered, 'Green.'

He then went on to ask me a series of questions about lighting and plug-point positioning and skirting and partial walls, and I listened to him, trying to see if he was giving any vocal cues as to which options he thought were best so I could just go with those. Sometimes I wouldn't even be listening. He would say something like, 'You probably want a gurgle fucker across that wall there', and I'd nod and say, 'Yeah, that is exactly what I was thinking.' And I do that every time, deferring to whatever they think, even if I did actually have an opinion on it.

'I was thinking of having it green, because it's a nice colour to work to.'

'Well, mate, we find a lot of clients like bl—'

'Yes, blue! Let's go with blue. I actually prefer blue.'

When they're doing the work, I hate having them in the house, because I'm obviously under the impression they're observing our behaviour so they can laugh about us later. I become nervous about using the toilet, I become worried that they're going to think I eat too much or that they're noting how much hot sauce I put on my food. I suddenly need the children to talk to me with more respect than they usually do so the builders I'm never going to see again think I'm a good father. I'm constantly offering them coffee and snacks as if I am catering a function, because I want these men to think I am a good builder host.

And then, finally, the grand unveiling, where I decide I have to be amazed by the work that's been done, even though I've been looking at it at the end of every day and it's exactly what I was expecting it to be. 'Wow, guys, I know we asked you to plaster the wall, but for it to be smooth and meet the absolute basic requirements of what the job entails, well, thank you so much!'

The worst, of course, is when the job goes wrong somehow. When this happens, I know Leesa is going to tell me I need to make a complaint, then she will watch me crumble like an arthritic meringue before losing her shit and stepping in because I am too pathetic.

We had a disaster with our office–garage-converter man, but then we decided he was good enough to do a load more work for us, one of those things being redoing our bathroom. He did the job fine, it seemed, then headed off. That evening we were watching TV in our room and Leesa was commenting on how I'd sounded even more amazed than usual about how good the bathroom looked, when we noticed an evil smell coming from it. Leesa immediately thought it was me, which I would have found insulting were it not for the fact that empirical evidence made that the most logical assumption.

It turned out it was coming from the shower, which was definitely not something we had asked for. I now started to get the sweats because I knew I was going to have to phone this man and try to get him to fix this fuck-up without charging me again, not because of the money, but because Leesa would kill me. If it was up to me I'd call and say, 'Hey, man, somebody really fucked up the shower after you left! Can we pay you to come fix it?'

The next day I made the call, and I'm almost embarrassed to tell you how this shit went down. He told me there was some issue with our plumbing that meant sewage smells would come up through our shower and nothing could be done about it. That sounds insane, right? I mean, unless I'm in Mumbai, that feels like a fairly unlikely scenario, doesn't it? Well, you can imagine how angry I was. I could have screamed and sworn at him for insulting me by thinking I would be so much of a moron as to accept that crap. I could have threatened legal action if he didn't come round and sort it out immediately. I could have even, in a fit of rage, threatened to smash his face in. What I actually did was thank him for his time. Genuinely: 'Sorry for bothering you, good to know.' I have no idea why – I was angry, but in that moment I wanted the conversation to end and the pressure and awkwardness of it made me believe that was a plausible explanation.

Suffice to say Leesa was unimpressed. Just last week, we got someone else in to undo what he had done and sort it all out. Leesa has asked me to get the original builder to pay for the work. I phoned him up straight away and demanded he pay the invoice with immediate effect or there would be consequences. I absolutely did not just pay it myself and lie to Leesa. I want to be absolutely clear on that.

Cars

There is such a disparity between how people feel in nice cars and how other people see them. I don't think it's possible to see a sports car race past you without looking up and thinking, 'Wanker!' I've lost count of the amount of times I've seen one drive by and imagined all that horse-power rattling around the tiny penis of whoever is at the wheel. I think this might be jealousy, but whatever it is, it's not the kind of thing I am willing to spend £100,000 on to inspire in other people.

It's only recently that I've really discovered how import-ant cars are to people, and in particular men. Cars are such a clear signal of how well you're doing in life, which is why men in particular find it so tempting to spend a shit load of money on them. You assume that people are going to admire you and women are going to desire you. In reality what mostly happens is that people say to each other: 'Did you see how ugly that man is driving that beautiful car?'

I passed my driving test relatively late at 24 years old. All my friends could drive pretty well by then, which meant that a running joke for a long time was that I drove like a grandma. This is indeed still true, but hasn't prevented me from having more than my fair share of accidents. I have, in my driving career, managed to write off three cars, two of them being Vauxhall Merivas, which tells you something about the amount of money I'm willing to spend on a vehicle. It also slightly undermines my assertion to the DVLA that my eyesight is good enough for me to be behind the wheel.

I remember on one night, while I was still a teacher, driving back from a gig at about 1 a.m. I was heading down the M1 when I encountered a series of cars strewn across the lanes in what looked like quite a nasty crash. I smashed into one of them (by accident) and had to pull over. When the police arrived, they asked me what I was doing out at that time. I explained that I was on my way back from a comedy gig. It was then that one of the police officers decided to share a story with me that he said I was welcome to use at one of my gigs. It was about going to his friend's house and finding a vibrator in the sink. I thanked him, assuming I would never use that story in my life. Turns out he was right and I was wrong. My apologies.

My car had to be towed away so Dad came to pick me up from the nearest service station. I fell asleep in the car, and woke to find him driving at about 120 mph. When I, in a panic, asked him why was driving so fast, he said he had assumed I wanted to get home as soon as possible, ignoring the possibility that I might be slightly shaken up by the multicar pile-up I had just been in. However, I guess there was some logic to his strategy, given I had to get to school in the morning.

The combination of my prejudice against drivers of flash cars and the fact that I have a tendency to destroy every car

I own has meant that I've never owned a particularly nice one. We bought a Volvo a few years ago because we thought that if I was likely to be driving, it was probably best to focus on the car with the best safety record. Leesa made a good go of talking about the car's other qualities, but I know that's why she wanted us to buy it.

It was when I was looking for a smaller car as a run-around that I became aware of how important cars are to the self-image of men. My friends all had strong opinions on what different cars said about you as a person. I suggested an Audi TT and my friends told me that people would assume I was on my way to give someone a cut and colour. I tried to impress them by suggesting I was going to get a Mercedes and they told me I would look like a chauffeur.

I am oversimplifying. The truth is, the assumptions they told me people would make based on the car I drive extended not only to the make but also to the model, the colour and even the specifications and features. They then had a lot of fun suggesting I should have a look at what women in their eighties were cruising around in because that would at least match my driving style.

There have indeed been occasions when people have judged me for the car I drive. I remember after a charity gig offering one of the other acts a lift in one of my pre-write-off Merivas. They genuinely could not believe the car I was driving. They kept saying things like, 'I thought you were doing OK? Why are you driving this piece of shit?' I don't even remember being embarrassed because Merivas are awesome.

In the end I stopped consulting my friends about what car to get. I even went through a phase of thinking it was too much of a minefield to bother getting anything. Then I found a discussion online and saw somebody say that driving a Mini was the closest thing you could get to experiencing Mario Kart in real life. So that's what I bought.

I remember my mum being devastated. Not for any concerns about my safety compared to the Volvo tank but because to her mind a Mini was not the sort of car that somebody who's on television should be driving. She was also worried about how I was going to get in and out of it. She thought I might get stuck inside. Fortunately that hasn't happened yet.

I love that Mini, partly because it does feel like driving a toy car. Recently, however, Freddie Flintoff has been trying to convince me to upgrade to something swankier. He's tried all sorts of arguments, like pointing out it makes sense for me to drive a flash car because I'm into hip-hop, and saying I worry too much about what people think. His main argument is that nice cars are worth the money because they are so much fun to drive. Fair enough, but I am very much of the opinion that if you can afford those cars when you are in your twenties, that's the time to drive them, because it's impressive and cool. What's not cool is being in your forties and driving around in a sports car like you're desperate to cheat on your wife.

Freddie was insistent, however. He told me that once I had tried driving a sports car, all my worries about looking like a show-off twat would disappear. I was becoming increasingly convinced, purely because of the fact that

Freddie Flintoff is about as far from a show-off as you can get, which I suppose is easy when you're brilliant at everything. He told me he would sort out a car I could borrow, and once I'd driven it for a bit he would wait for my apology. I didn't at any point bring up the fact that there was no fucking way I could ever justify spending the kind of money the cars he had in mind would cost.

Sure enough, true to his word, I received a phone call a few days later confirming that I would be taking delivery of a Porsche Carrera for the week. I'll be honest, I was fairly excited about the possibility of spending the week driving the nicest car I have ever been in. That was combined, however, with a series of fears, which ranged from the neighbours visiting Leesa to offer her support through my midlife crisis, to me driving the Porsche for about 15 minutes before it went the way of one of my beloved Merivas.

I didn't feel much better when it arrived and it was bright yellow. Leesa started laughing in a way that suggested that seeing me in the car was not going to be the turn-on I hoped it would. Why the fuck was it yellow!? I couldn't believe it. I was already feeling nervous about looking like an attention-seeker and now I had become convinced that midway through my first drive there would be a Crawley Twitter trend called #Bananacunt.

I don't think I have ever reversed a car more slowly off a driveway than I did that Porsche. The prospect of having to explain to my neighbour that I had crashed my borrowed penis extension into their house just didn't bear thinking about.

I managed to navigate my street without any issues and

then I was out on the open road. I'll be absolutely honest with you, and I don't know if you've driven one of these cars, but they sound unbelievable. I found myself understanding the Jeremy Clarkson-style excitement the roar of the engine can incite. After driving the car for a little while I even started feeling a bit xenophobic.

I knew that I had to give my mum a lift in it. On the way over, it became clear to me that driving a sports car does not make you a more adventurous driver. I had anticipated getting stares of envy and even possibly of sexual arousal. What I hadn't anticipated was getting puzzled stares from people wondering why a man was driving a Porsche like it was a Toyota Prius. If anything, I was driving even more slowly than usual because I was freaking out so much about damaging it.

It is fair to say that my mum, when she saw the car, lost her shit. 'This is the car you should be driving! It is not embarrassing like that Mini!' She got into the car, pretending that the incredibly low seat hadn't made that a struggle, then asked me to drive around all of the places where it was most likely her friends would see us. We drove through town, we drove past her work, we spent a good portion of time just driving past her friends' houses. I totally understand where Mum was coming from. She was just being a proud mum and ignoring the fact that I had only been allowed to borrow the car because of my friend and that it was not a sign of any kind of achievement on my part.

I can't deny we had a great time, but I would go as far as to say I found the whole thing slightly embarrassing. Part of the problem is you're not driving the sports car around

Monaco. You're pulling the sports car into the car park at the local garden centre to take your mum for a coffee. What made it worse was that my mum took loads of photos of us in the car and posted them on Facebook, giving the impression I had just bought it. The comments below were things like, 'I see Romesh has become one of them now, has he?' I found it excruciating, but held back from explaining the truth because, well, that looks a little bit desperate, doesn't it?

So, despite enjoying driving the Porsche, and thinking it's a fantastic car (a desperate plug in case anyone would like to give me a free one), I concluded that a vehicle that nice makes sense for a car fanatic like Freddie, but not for a car heathen like me. Driving round in a Porsche just doesn't work for a fat dad of three in Crawley. Having said that, I have asked Freddie if he could hook me up with a loan car every week for the rest of my life.

Dancing

I cannot remember the last time I danced. I think I retired from the activity but didn't feel it necessary to make an announcement. I've left it so long now that there's going to be a huge amount of pressure on me next time I do dance. However, this is probably only going to happen if I'm the victim of a hostage situation where I have to dance to save my family, and even then I wouldn't move my arms much.

Men beyond a certain age dancing is a disgusting thing to watch. I know there are exceptions, and there are certain cultures where dancing is important and so they can throw down, but in general it is a horrible blowtorch to the dignity. Many men would do well to abstain from it in the same way people give up smoking and saturated fat. I have horrific memories of seeing my dad at parties doing the 'checking my shoes for dogshit' dance, sweating his arse off while my mum danced with him. What made it even more tragic is that every now and again he would have to stop to wipe some sweat from his forehead, and I'd feel the immense relief of thinking he'd finished, only to realize he was merely taking a break before going back to it.

It may be the memories of this that have made me so

terrified of dancing, which is weird for someone who listens to music so much. Self-consciousness is the enemy of dancing. When I first did *Mock The Week*, one of the jokes I told during 'Scenes We'd Like to See' was, 'She danced like nobody was watching, but people were watching and she looked like a twat.' That joke came from my soul. Whenever there's an occasion where dancing is required, part of me is convinced it's some sort of huge prank and midway through twerking, the music will stop, everybody will point and laugh, and Leesa and the kids will have to distance themselves from me permanently as the only way they can continue to lead normal lives.

I do go to a lot of music gigs, and I do move to the music, but mainly because it looks weirder to stand there completely rigid. But I approach it with trepidation if I'm with people who haven't seen me dance before, or who I haven't seen move either. There's something really weird about seeing somebody you know dance for the first time. You have no idea what their level of competence is, and you find out almost immediately. The worst discovery is that they combine a complete lack of rhythm with really committing to the moves, which means you are going to be associated with a car crash. Of course, you don't say anything, because telling people to stop dancing is unforgivable. You just have to slowly move away from them. There is something about dancing that we consider holy – 'He's just enjoying himself!' – and that makes it impossible to criticize. People even find bad dancing endearing. But I don't want that politeness. I want to know if I'm making a fool of myself. If I'm at a gig getting a bit too carried away, I want a friend who taps me on the shoulder and says, 'Mate, I'm really sorry, but your dancing is so bad it's actually funnier than your last tour.' I'd be mortified but I'd rather know. Then again, to avoid that distinct possibility, I have largely taken myself out of the dancing game. I've even contemplated taking a crutch to every gig or party so I can feign injury.

I have had so many bad experiences dancing. All the times I tried to dance with a woman only to have her run away mean that I associate the act itself with rejection. I would point out at this juncture that I'm delighted this dance-flirting ritual seems to have gone away as acceptable behaviour. It was apparently fine to dance up to a girl you liked the look of, bumping and grinding, and she would have to run the risk of being accused of being up herself if she rejected this unprovoked approach. I found the whole thing unbearable, as they never had the lights down low enough in these places for me to look attractive. I'd have much preferred a system where you all wear your email address on your shirt and if you like someone you can email them with your photo and a suggestion to meet up, and they can either respond or not, and nobody has to feel bad. You are, of course, going to get people who group-email everybody, but no system is perfect, and someone who looks like me would absolutely have to do that just on the basis of probability.

I remember on one occasion going out with a mate who introduced me to his group of friends, one of whom was a very attractive girl. I talked to her with no agenda and we got on brilliantly, although it's possible she saw me as an asexual creature she would never consider as a romantic option. Nevertheless, I was pleasantly surprised that we were getting on and even flirting. I was being extremely funny, or at least she was pretending I was, and my friends were looking at each other in surprise – the same look I imagine you would give your dog if it started talking.

The problem came when we arrived at the club. We went in and got drinks and were chatting by the bar when everyone decided they wanted to hit the dancefloor. I thought nothing of it at the time but now I realize it was a ploy by my companions to ruin my evening. I initially resisted the dancefloor, hoping I could encourage this girl to stay and chat ('No agenda, Romesh?'), but eventually she suggested we dance. That would normally be good news, and indeed I thought it was. I was going to dance like a don, she would see I was as silky with the moves as I was with the chat, and we would kiss and my friends could fucking suck it. That was the plan.

As we made our way to the floor, there came the issue of when you actually start dancing. You either head in already dancing, which leads to potential embarrassment and maximum exposure, or you walk normally to where you decide your spot is going to be and then you begin from a standing start, which looks insane. I opted for walking behind her and letting her take the lead. We arrived at a spot in the centre of the floor and she moved from walking into dancing naturally and seamlessly. I followed suit and got ready to dance the night away and make my friends rue the fucking day they ever doubted me.

As she saw me dancing, she did not recoil in horror. She

did something much worse. She laughed. But it wasn't an 'Aren't you shit at dancing?' laugh. It was worse than that. It was a laugh that suggested she thought I was dancing like that to be funny. She thought she was being nice by laughing at my funny joke-dancing. Except that was me really trying to dance. Oh God. This was a situation that even with my level of failure I hadn't seen before. I decided to get into a different dance move immediately to show that the funny bit was at an end. Sadly, this was greeted with even more laughter than the previous one. This was now an issue. Most people only have about four dances they can choose between, and based on the fact she found my favourite two fucking hilarious, I was pretty sure the third one wasn't going to be less comedic. Not only was this situation unsalvageable, I also had to try and make sure I never saw this woman again. I did not want to be at a wedding at some point in the future and hear cackling as she recounts to her friends that she can't believe she's seen me again and my dancing is as hilarious as she remembered. I had no choice but to pretend I needed the toilet and leave immediately. Sadly I couldn't leave as we were miles from home so instead I just stopped talking to her. She may have found it weird but I thought that was the better option than saying, 'My dancing there was how I actually dance and so I've realized we can never be happy together, I'm sorry.'

Being a hardcore hip-hop fan isn't conducive to dancing either. When people think of hip-hop they think of b-boys and breaking, but my experience of dancing to hip-hop is standing in a circle with your friends and rapping really aggressively to each other. I had no idea how fucking idiotic this looks. Nevertheless, that was exclusively the type of dancing we did for years. It was insane. We'd go to a club, scream lyrics at each other and then wonder why we'd come home alone again. We did it over and over again until eventually one of my friends said, 'Guys, we look like an absolute bunch of dickheads.' We looked around and all agreed, as did everyone else in the club, I imagine.

The other occasion you find yourself dancing is at a wedding. Thankfully, save for some inevitable Thai bride dalliances in a couple of my friends' futures, I am beyond attending weddings. I am amazed that any men who have attended and danced at a wedding ever have sex again. It is a car crash of rhythm-devoid gyrating that is a real advert for men's dancing being made illegal.

And so I have realized that I do not dance any more. I am beyond being required to by social pressure and I'm pretty sure all of my friends know where I stand (without moving). I'm taking this opportunity to encourage you, if you are a guy, to also stop dancing in public. If you feel you must dance, please do so in the privacy of your own home when nobody is watching. Unless you have some skills, nobody needs to see that shit.

Lockdown

As I write this, people are beginning to wind down certain measures of the coronavirus lockdown. I say people, rather than the government, because as soon as the government started with that Stay Alert crap, everybody decided they were going to come up with their own interpretations of the rules. I do not want to alienate any of you with a political diatribe. There may be some of you who believe the government have absolutely nailed the handling of this Covid crisis, and you are entitled to your opinion, and I would never judge you for being the fucking idiots you clearly are.

I jest, of course. The truth is none of us truly know how well the government have done because most of us do not have a clue how to deal with a global pandemic. At the beginning of lockdown, no longer able to talk crap at the pub, my friends and I initiated Zoom social chats, before realizing they were fucking awful. I always found it funny when somebody started pontificating on what the government should do. They always seemed to be incredibly passionate, and my response would be, 'Yes, you're probably right' rather than, 'Do you mind telling me why any of us is supposed to attach any credibility to the medical opinions of someone who works in insurance?'

I am no expert but I would say this – everyone thought the government were screwing it up, then they relaxed the lockdown and everyone seems pretty happy again. Turns out all we needed to beat this virus was a sunny weekend and readily available booze. I have no idea how this is going to pan out, and it's possible that this book will end up documenting the run-up to the end of days as people decided that going to Bournemouth was more important than protecting our vulnerable. You're probably reading this on a screen because they had to use all the printing equipment for 'How To Deal With The Apocalypse' flyers.

It has been an interesting thing to process, being on lockdown. To my mind it has shone a light on how our stresses and activities are just made up. Many people had their jobs stop with immediate effect, and ended up struggling to find some sort of purpose. It was a challenge, mentally, which is probably why you had so many people doing mad shit at home. Entertainers have come out of this whole thing pretty badly – they haven't dealt with their decreased relevance particularly well. I include myself in this, someone who thought it would be a good idea to do daily Facebook Lives with absolutely zero content, so essentially there are now about forty hours of me being utterly boring. I've lost count of the number of times I've seen Gary Barlow and friends duetting on Skype. If the government really wants to help the creative sector, they need to provide some sort of service for singers, actors and musicians where they will purge from existence anything you did during lockdown. Even now, as I think back to the beginning of this whole period, it was like a kind of madness descended on public figures. Celebrities would go live on Instagram and publicly broadcast their break-down. Madonna confirmed she was batshit for the last three people in the world who still thought she might be normal, and I even thought about doing an online cook-ing show with my mum. I mean, what the fuck was going on?! That all seems like insanity now. I feel like I've just woken up from a massive night out, and I'm lying in bed with all the videos I made during lockdown, regretting every single one of my actions.

Some real reflection has happened, however. Before I say what I am about to say, please know that I think the pandemic has been absolutely horrendous and my heart goes out to the families who have been rocked by it, and all this talk about a possible second spike means it's entirely possible I'm dead now. But the lockdown really has been a revelatory experience – never again will we spend so much unadulterated time with our loved ones. I know that has meant many times when you have wanted to batter the shit out of every last one of them, but it has been pretty amazing as well. I for one have realized that spending time with my kids needs to be a bigger priority and so I have booked time off in the future and planned trips so that we can continue to have longer chunks of time together, which we are lucky to be able to do. I have also come to appreciate, around the long sections of time when hearing each other breathe feels rage-inducing, that spending time with my wife is probably a good thing – either it will solid-ify our relationship or confirm we should split up, and either outcome is useful to get to.

Equally, I have found myself making proper contact with my mum. By that I mean calling her and properly engaging with her because I have the time to do so, rather than calling her on the way to doing something and being abrupt and half listening, which is my normal position. In life pre-virus, I lost count of the number of times I asked my mum a question about something she had literally just been talking about, properly highlighting that I was not paying attention.

That seems to be the experience of a lot of my friends too. During the times they've been able to process the obvious trauma of what's happening, this experience has enabled them to have a real look at what they are doing with their lives and reflect on their priorities going forward. I mean, that's what they're all saying now. The reality is that three weeks after being let loose we will all be back to doing exactly what we were doing before and I will be paying as much attention to my mum's conversation as Donald Trump does to the welfare of Mexican children.

When the lockdown began, loads of people started declaring what they were going to do when it was over. They were going to have mad nights out, and hug everyone, and treasure what we had been refitted with. People were saying that because they thought the virus would be stopped in its tracks and lockdown would end with immediate effect. We all assumed Boris would hold a press conference where he would smash a giant ice sculpture of the coronavirus and say, 'We've beaten it, motherfuckers! Get yourselves amongst it' and there would be three consecutive national holidays for everyone just to have a massive rave-up. At the time of writing, what has actually happened is we haven't sorted anything, the virus is still out there, but we've realized it's not going to be a quick win and we need to live our lives again, so we are limping back towards normal service. You are allowed to go to the pub, but you can only stay for three drinks and you have to plan what you're having before you arrive. You can go to the theatre, but they're not allowed to put any performances on. Theme parks are open, but not any of the fun rides. It's mad. But the worst part is we're not going to have this hedonist post-corona orgasm that every-body was imagining.

Still, the biggest false dawn of lockdown for me has been video calls. I love them and hate them in equal measure. Obviously, they are awkward as fuck, with 50 per cent of conversations consisting of people waiting for other people to talk, as well as saying, 'No, you go' about a thou-sand times.

I will tell you this, though – they are going to have to provide some pretty incredible snacks if anyone wants me to ever leave my house for a meeting again. We've all real-ized that 90 per cent of meetings are a complete waste of time, not to mention the time we spend travelling to and from them. I have just done a second series of *The Ranga-nation*. For the first series, I would travel to Shepherd's Bush to spend the day writing and then come home after gigging the stuff at a local comedy club, which would mean leaving my house at 8 a.m. and returning at about 11 p.m. For this series, I would do the writing on a Zoom call, starting my laptop up at 10 while eating my breakfast, before doing an online gig from the same room at 8, and be done and ready for lovemaking at 9 p.m. Plus I haven't had to scream at a Southern Rail worker for something that wasn't their fault.

The weirdest phenomenon of the lockdown was our sudden decision to become quizzers. I've never enjoyed quizzes in my life, mainly because it's a social event with a definite finish time, which makes me feel like a prisoner. Regardless of this, I have taken part in at least ten quizzes over the last three months, deriving almost no joy from any of them, save for the happiness you glean from one of the other couples having an argument.

My friends and I also all decided we were going to have our aforementioned regular pub nights on Zoom. What an absolute fucking shitshow that was. Sitting in your living room and enduring a conversation that veered between awkward silence and everyone talking over everyone, never reaching a happy medium. You would find yourself having to repeat an off-the-cuff joke after the moment had passed and then wait for someone to say they wish they had a tumbleweed function on Zoom.

The other issue with lockdown socializing is you can't fucking leave. At least when you're out you can make up an excuse to escape or get off when the night is looking a bit shit. Sometimes you want to get out early if it turns out to be a proper dud, but you can't make up an emergency when people can see your house isn't actually on fire. I don't back my acting skills sufficiently to be able to say to somebody: 'OK, you can't see it because it's behind the laptop, but three armed men have just broken in. No, they've signalled to me that they don't want us to turn the laptop around to show you, and they said if you call the police they will kill us and then find you and kill you. We should probably log off. Let us know when you're doing this again!'

The people I really feel sorry for are the future children of our kids now, who are going to have to endure stories of how tough lockdown was and how they should consider themselves lucky they're even allowed to go outside and sit in a McDonald's. The stories will be so exaggerated – lockdown will have gone on for three years, and you wouldn't have been allowed to buy food at all, you had to rely on airdropped rations, which would never contain toilet paper, leading to the toilet-roll conflict of March 2020. They will be forced to watch endless documentaries about it at school and eventually there will be some sort of lockdown remembrance day.

The face mask has been an interesting lockdown phenomenon. I have absolutely no idea as to the efficacy of wearing one because we don't seem to have any clear information as to how good they may or may not be. When this whole thing started, everyone was saying they were pointless, including people in the medical profession. Then it started being suggested that maybe it was a good idea to wear them. Then it was suggested that people think about wearing them, until eventually it was decided they were compulsory.

Whether you think they are a good idea or not, and I would hazard a guess that for most of you reading this, that opinion is based purely on fact-free information, I think we can all agree that going into Tesco with everyone in masks is really fucking weird. It feels like you're in an apocalypse film, except you can still get tiger bread.

The resistance of people to wearing face masks is something I find baffling. I get they're uncomfortable, and I get that the policy on them has been unclear to say the least, but I do not understand the rebellion. At the time of writing, it's been made mandatory. Just wear it, mate. I realize you might not agree with it. I don't agree with people being allowed to torture animals on *I'm a Celebrity* but I have accepted it. This isn't a great example actually, as I'm continually expressing my opposition to this, and refuse to watch the show as a result. I just feel sorry for the people working in these shops, obliged to implement a measure which puts them into contact with lunatics claiming it's a violation of their civil rights to be forced to wear a mask to buy Hob-Nobs. It reminds me of my time as a school teacher when I would have to tell kids to tuck their shirts in despite not giving a shit if they were tucked in or not. They would ask me why, and I would have no answer. If I was teaching now, I think I would probably make up something about untucked shirts being known to spread some sort of virus.

It is difficult to know what the long-term effects of this pandemic will be. I kind of suspect that we will discover the virus would have run its course regardless and this was a massive waste of fucking time. It will have been worth it, though, to discover that I can socialize with my mum on Zoom – if only she could figure out how to use it.

Mental Health

Mental health has become such a trendy thing to talk about that I'm almost reluctant to bring it up. I think there's no doubt that having some sort of mental-health issue is pretty fashionable. I would much rather that, however, than have us stay in the situation where mental health is stigmatized and people feel embarrassed to talk about it.

It's a difficult one, isn't it? There are people in the world worried about whether they're going to be killed by their own government. I'm not sure they would have much sympathy for somebody complaining to a therapist that they got a lot of nasty tweets about their last sitcom. But that attitude isn't helpful. It's like saying that we shouldn't go to the doctor about a persistent cough because there are people who don't have any legs.

I feel strongly that being on top of your mental health is such a driver of basic happiness that it should be part of the national curriculum. I reckon that, for a lot of kids, learning how to manage stress and self-doubt is probably a lot more useful than adding fractions with different denominators. Teachers already do a bit of counselling. Encouraging a child to see the act of struggling with a maths problem or a new concept as part of the learning process, rather than something to get stressed out about, is equipping children with valuable skills, but it's not enough.

I have to be honest. When I was a teacher, I would be so desperate for the lesson not to go down the toilet that when a kid misbehaved my first thought wouldn't be, 'I must help that child manage the set of emotions that got them to exhibit this behaviour.' I would think, 'How do I get this kid to shut the fuck up?' But now I'm out of that pressure cooker I genuinely think children should be taught more about managing stress and dealing with sadness, and should be shown coping mechanisms for dealing with periods of adversity.

I have seen the absence of this in my own kids. I'll see one of them getting stuck on a videogame and losing their shit. They start saying that the game is designed for them to fail, and then when it gets really bad they may even throw the controller in some sort of rage. I do think they should be helped with how to process all that, and of course the responsibility lies with parents. When the kids lash out, I know I should say something like, 'Could you please explain to me why it is you feel so angry with the game? Is it because there is something stressing you out at home that has led you to feel like that? Shall we sit down and discuss proper strategies for helping to deal with these feelings in the future?'

What I actually say is: 'Are you shitting me? Do you have any idea how much these controllers cost? The next time you break a controller there is absolutely no way I'm replacing it.'

If it isn't already clear, I'm absolutely not nailing the whole 'teach your children how to be resilient' thing.

I mean, look: it's possible that a child throwing a controller is just part of life. It's no big deal, and talking about it as a problem is arguably another sign of how much we wrap children in cotton wool. After all, I myself used to throw controllers when I played video games as a child. My counter argument to that would be, first, I have had to receive mental-health support for most of my adult life, and secondly, controllers really are fucking expensive.

Anyway, what I'm trying to say is that a conversation like that shouldn't be a big deal. You don't need to hold a therapy session every time a child has a tantrum. But it should be something that's spoken about. I really feel that checking in on someone's mental health should be as normal as talking about going to the gym. On the tour before last my preparation to go onstage consisted of little more than watching Netflix right up until the point I was due to walk out. While I thought this was OK at the time, I found those shows stressful and mentally exhausting. On my latest tour, a friend recommended I try meditation.

Now, for all my talk about making mental health a normal topic of conversation, I do find the idea of meditation a little bit 'hippy bollocks'. The idea that, as busy as we are, you would take time out of your day to sit there doing absolutely nothing and not even really getting any rest. It's worse than sleeping in terms of doing fuck all, because at least sleeping is beneficial. Regardless of my reservations, I did try to do it. I tried the Headspace app. This is where a man with a voice that is annoying enough to take you out of the meditation guides you through the process. He says things like, 'Focus on the sounds in the room, think about where your legs are, remember you have hands.' It is supposed to encourage you to exist completely in the moment. My problem is that my mind wanders and I start thinking things like, 'What would I put in my dream curry?' Or 'I wonder if Leesa knows that I masturbate?' Apparently, however, that happens to everyone, although perhaps not those specific questions, and you are, in the Headspace man's words, supposed to gently bring your mind back into the room.

I don't know what you thought when you read that paragraph. You might have thought, that sounds absolutely wonderful, and you can't wait to give it a try. On the other hand, you might have thought that sounds like the biggest waste of time imaginable. All I can tell you is that once I got past the creeping paranoia that somebody might be watching me doing this, I started to find it beneficial. There is something about tapping out on your day-to-day worries for just ten minutes that makes them seem a lot more manageable. I would highly recommend it, although I can't imagine my demeanour makes me a very good advert for the whole thing.

My fear of being spied on comes from, I think, a specific incident from my childhood. I loved the song 'Guerrillas In The Mist' by Da Lench Mob. It was one of those songs that, if you rapped along to it, you would feel like an absolute badman. Now, of course, this kind of behaviour is actively encouraged on TikTok, and you can actually make a living from it. Back in my day, however, you had to settle for doing it in your bedroom alone. On one particular day, I was feeling in the mood for some mirror rapping, so I grabbed a hairbrush and started really going for it. It's a particularly aggressive song, and for the full effect I would suggest you listen to it after reading this little anecdote. As you're listening, imagine a tubby little brown boy trying to convey the rage of the disenfranchised black male in southern California. As I came to the end of the last verse of the song, it was midway through my aggressive head nods to close out the number that I noticed one of my brother's friends watching me through the crack in the door.

You know in the film *Spiderman* when he gets bitten by the spider and then you see all his cells merge with spider stuff to give him superpowers? Well, that is what happened to me, except that the spider stuff was shame. I was humiliated. So humiliated, in fact, that I didn't proffer any kind of excuse. I might as well have turned to him and said, 'Do with that information what you will.' That episode alone has left me with an ongoing 'shame sense', again a little bit like Spiderman, where whenever I'm doing something slightly embarrassing I'm convinced somebody's watching me. I guess that also explains the Leesa-knowing-I-masturbate question. I hesitate to call it a superpower.

When you think about it, you are most miserable when you are worrying about things. When you are experiencing tragedy or disaster, you deal with it. It's when you think about it that the sadness really kicks in. There is an argument, therefore, that being taught how to process these things is one of the most important life skills you could have. When my dad died, the repercussions took me years to work through. I had to seek help. I sought out counselling, but it took me a while to accept that that was what I needed to do. When we are ill, we know to go to the doctor or to hospital. We put our physical health rightly at the top of our priorities, and I really think that we should be doing the same for our mental health. I'm not even convinced that most people have a proper awareness of what their state of mental health is. I genuinely believe one of the main factors to being happy is the manner in which we process what happens to us, and that is best managed through being on top of your mental health. That sounds almost profound, but the truth is I have performed the age-old trick of listening to a lot of opinions of people more important than myself and combining them to pass off as my own.

I'm convinced there must be a way for us to step into adulthood far better equipped for things like that. Our mental health is always going to come under strain at points in our lives, and men are arguably worse than women at addressing things that prey on our minds. Suicide is still the biggest killer of men under forty-five, which is a terrifying statistic. Is it possible that we could emerge from school knowing a bit less about the Romans and a bit more about ourselves? I mean, no disrespect to History teachers but a lot of this shit is googleable.

I think that's more important now than it ever was. When I was at school, I once left my judo suit in the class-room. The next day my form teacher held up the judo suit to ask if anyone wanted to claim it, and also pointed out that it had skid marks on it. I really did not want to claim that judo suit, but at the same time I did not want to do judo with no trousers on. In hindsight I should have just told my mom I had lost them and got some new ones. Unfortunately, they don't have 'get yourself out of embarrassing social situations' on the national curriculum either, although in this instance a simple lesson in wiping your arse properly may have sufficed. The insensitivity of my form teacher aside, that really was humiliating. However, it does freak me out that if that happened to one of my children now the repercussions would be so much worse. There is a good chance that their skid judo bottoms would become some sort of meme. At the very least, everyone at their school would receive an immediate text alert. I think the point I'm trying to make is that kids today are probably under greater scrutiny and far more mental stress than we ever were, but I think maybe the takeaway from this is let's all just make sure that our anal hygiene is on point.

Religion

The idea of religion and whether or not there is a God is something I have spent a lot of time thinking about, largely because my upbringing in an admittedly relaxed religious home has sat in deep contrast to my experiences at school and in adult life.

When I was a kid, my parents used to take us to a Hindu temple in Wembley every weekend. I used to love it, mainly because we would get Sri Lankan takeaway on the way home, but I did also enjoy being at the temple itself. It was filled with incredible-looking Hindu deities and there were fabulously dressed priests who would do prayers for you if you requested them, in Sanskrit, which I had assumed only my brother and I didn't understand but it turns out my parents didn't either.

My mum and dad prayed frequently; we had a shrine room in our house, which was basically a cupboard filled with pictures of various gods, including a tiny statue of Ganesh, which my mum gave to me and I have in my house to this day. They also encouraged us to pray and my mum in particular would threaten us that God wouldn't like certain things we were doing.

What my parents never did was explain what our

religion was, and what its fundamental tenets were. I think they assumed that we would take it on board through osmosis, but I grew up only knowing that God was someone to pray to and he would kick our arses if we did anything wrong. I became so convinced about the punishment system that if anything went wrong, from me banging my head to failing an exam to having an argument with a friend, I would rack my brains to think of what I had done to deserve it – it's not a particularly great way of avoiding paranoia, although I'm not going to blame Hinduism for what was much more likely placed in my psyche by smoking copious amounts of marijuana. I do remember feeling, when my dad went to prison and my parents split up, that God must be really angry with us. (For more on that episode, you'll just have to read my first book, *Straight Outta Crawley*.)

Stand-up comedy, particularly in Britain, is pretty dismissive about religion and the people that follow it, and even the religious comics talk around it a lot on stage and rarely address the existence of God. I myself have spoken about it, citing the fact that we haven't really seen much evidence of God recently. I pointed out that, as you get older and you become aware of the sense that the world is in complete chaos, the idea that this is all part of some master plan becomes increasingly difficult to swallow.

What makes it even less convincing is the fact that, as a construct, it's the perfect way to control people's actions. If you were looking to engage in some sort of mass behavioural management, because you have noticed that people are getting really jealous of each other's donkeys, religion would be a great way to go about it. You set up a list of rules that absolutely must be obeyed and you have people believe that if they don't obey these rules they will be punished for all eternity, which is far more punitive than any prison even a tired and hungry Donald Trump could come up with.

The strict rules and the punishment of misdeeds does undermine the inherent belief that religious people are better or nicer than everyone else, if you follow the logic to its ultimate conclusion. If somebody is nice to you and they believe in God, they are being kind because they are led by the idea they need to behave in a certain way in order to get into heaven. It's like somebody coming to your rescue when you're getting mugged and then finding out the only reason they stepped in is because they were promised a car. If an atheist comes by to help you, then they really just want to help you. They are not doing it to get a better view in heaven.

I find it difficult to envision exactly what heaven is. Now, that is a statement bordering on the arrogant – the obvious counterargument is, 'How could you possibly understand the enormity and complexity of God's heaven with your pathetic human mind?', and I do honestly get all that. It is just very difficult for me to understand how we'd all be living happily together in heaven when our tastes are so markedly different. Surely my heaven would be considerably different to yours. Leesa and I very rarely even agree on what box set to watch, so the idea that we would be spending eternity together, both happy in the same environment and never finding anything to argue about, feels far-fetched. What if Leesa really isn't that into me and is staying with me for the sake of giving the children what she perceives to be a fully rounded family upbringing? Surely she deserves release from that after she dies? Do we all become single again when we die? I understand that I'm being wilfully ignorant here and my views are grounded in my earthly conscience and we will have no want of box sets in heaven, but it is a tricky proposition to sell something as abstract as an incentive for spending your whole life living as purely as you can. I imagine it was an easier sell when your life expectancy was thirty and you spent most of it with violent dysentery. Now that we are all living much longer and we have things like the Marvel movie universe and curry delivery, it is more difficult to persuade people to disengage with the immediate pleasures of life.

One of the problems people have with the religious is that they go on about their faith too much. I completely disagree – I don't think they go on about it nearly enough. Don't get me wrong, I don't want to get preached at the whole time, but look at it from the religious person's point of view. They think everyone else is going to hell for permanent and incessant damnation. And, by the sounds of it, damnation is not something you get used to in the way you get adjusted to a bath being slightly too hot. It is a fresh day of shit every single time, assuming they even work only by day – it's highly possible they go 24 hours, one of many things that hell has in common with Tesco. If they truly believe this, shouldn't they be telling everybody all the time? I have friends who are religious, which means they think I might be damned if I don't see the light – why the fuck are we talking about football? If I knew you could get a free holiday, I would not stop telling everybody I knew until they had all booked, and I'd even go round telling strangers – and that's just a fortnight in Portugal. We are talking about eternal damnation!

I mean, I am a moron talking through arguments that far more intelligent people than I have pondered for a much longer time, but these are the arguments that have swirled around in my head over and over. Asian culture places a lot of importance on spirituality, as it also does on getting a good education and making yourself some decent wedge, which I have always found slightly contradictory as religion is very much about detaching yourself from the material spoils of this life.

Having given my GCSE-level arguments for why I am dubious about religion, I feel I should also consider all the reasons that I really want to be wrong about it. First of all, having unshakeable faith in anything is something to be envious of, although I realize that in itself is a sin. Secondly, to have a belief that gives you confidence that life is all part of a plan must be incredibly reassuring when faced with things as distressing as a global pandemic or the ongoing survival of Katie Hopkins.

Also, I find the idea that this is as good as it gets, that this is the peak of existence, slightly depressing. People as individuals are great, but as a worldwide population there is little to suggest we are making a good fist of this whole life thing. If there is a God, I can only imagine he is looking at the situation in the same way that you might look at your garage when you decide it needs a massive clear-out – you have a good look at it, decide it's probably too big a job to really even start and convince yourself you will come back to it later. I find it hard to believe that God is looking at what's going on here at the moment and thinking, 'That looks pretty much in order, no reason to get involved.'

The biggest pitfall of being an atheist, of course, is being an atheist. I find it incredible that vegans get the amount of stick they do for banging on about it when atheists exist. If there is a more self-satisfied section of society, then – well, I was about to say I'd love to see it, but the truth is I'd love to be kept the hell away from them.

Considering that atheists believe it to be blindingly obvious that there is no God, they love to have a discussion about it. Atheists love getting into some sort of intellectual debate about why there is no God, eternally hoping that they will convert someone away from their faith and get them to join their travelling band of smug arseholes.

So, I still haven't reached a definitive conclusion. But I do think it's probably best to follow the argument of Pascal's wager, which is that if you are unsure, go with the existence of God. All you have to do is pray and attend some social gatherings, maybe get circumcised depending on your sex and which one you're going for, and you could potentially avoid hell and have an amazing time choosing whatever box set you like for ever. On the other hand, if you decide to go atheist, and you're right about the absence of an afterlife, well, the only real reward is the people you know not having to listen to you bang on about it any more.

Social Media

Remove yourself from all social media with immediate effect. That is my very clear advice to you. I have not taken it myself, but I have become increasingly convinced that it is the only way forward. I have to admit I'm slightly addicted to it, but there are positives – it is a way of keeping abreast of sports, news and pop culture, and without it, sitting on the toilet would feel like an eternity. On the other hand, the negative effects of it can be far-reaching, time-consuming and mental-health eating.

For a while I had been of the opinion that Facebook was the nice one – you are friends with the people you want to be, and you are able to keep up with their news and lives. I have now come to the conclusion that it can be problematic. First, the obvious consideration over how people present the positive sides of themselves and you find yourself in competition with their impossibly perfect lives. We post a photo of our children with brand new haircuts and people comment on how smart they look and how nice it is that they get on, without realizing they had to be bribed to do the photo and one of them stabbed the hairdresser with her own scissors.

The other thing that has become prevalent across all

social media, which I find absolutely unacceptable, is brag-
ging. It started off as a bit of humblebragging, but now we
have freed ourselves from the shackles of that and seem to
think it's OK to just baldly demand that people recognize
how wonderful we are. I've lost count of the number of
posts on my timeline that say things like: 'Just finished
unpacking our stuff in our new house. Bottle of champagne
to celebrate. So proud of how far we have come this year.'

I'm sorry, what? It's disgusting to flaunt your happiness in
front of everyone in such a brazen way. What happened to
the good old-fashioned British way of moaning about how
shit things are to make other people feel better: 'Just moved
into our new place. One of the removals guys smashed half
our crockery while being pretty racist and we've already discovered that one of the rooms has damp.' Now, that's the
kind of post I can get behind – I've been informed you have
a new house plus I know that stuff is going wrong with it so
I don't feel so bad about the fact we've lived in the same
house for years and still don't have curtains.

Far worse than the lifestyle boast is the phenomenon of
declaring your good deeds on Facebook. Here people also
take the shameless decision to try to pass off even posting
about it as a good deed, rather than the advert it obviously
is for what a good person they are: 'Just gave a homeless
person a bit of cash and stopped for a chat. Took just a
little bit of my time but so so worth it. Hope some of you
will take this as an incentive to maybe have a go yourself.'
Oh, fuck off, mate. I have spoken to you, and it would
have been far more humane to have given that person the
money without also forcing your conversation on them.

Facebook might be a stage for self-importance, but Twitter and Instagram are time sponges I just can't see the benefits of, despite me being on them a lot. I have been forced to stop engaging with people on Twitter because it has become too combative. Twitter is a sea of opinion effluent, filled with horrific people exclusively searching for things and people they hate so they can be vile to them. I receive almost daily messages from people that go, 'I usually find you funny but I had to get in touch to say that I thought the show was offensive and shit tonight.' That statement is everything that is wrong with Twitter. People are very happy to enjoy something quietly, but as soon as they dislike or disagree with you they feel obliged to express themselves. The entire platform is fuelled by negativity.

This extends to the way people speak to women when they can hide behind the relative anonymity of a Twitter handle. Occasionally I've been tagged in tweets alongside female comics and I don't think a single one of those posts has remained untainted by someone commenting on the fact they either find them fit or they really don't. I've been guilty in the past of thinking that men get this abuse too, because of messages I've received about being overweight or having a wonky eye, but that was before I realized that women get some sort of rank shit on each and every post, so much so that when I mention something specific to a female friend they often don't know what I'm referring to. If you're a man and you've ever felt compelled to comment on how hot a woman is on Twitter, I genuinely believe you should be neutered.

There is an argument that, as a public figure, it's a good

thing to be communicating on social media, but the idea that anyone can get hold of you is not so good. I get messages from people who become furious that I haven't replied to them. I had one encounter recently where a man started by asking me to do him a personalized video, then messaged again to ask if I had seen the request, then messaged a third time to ask why I hadn't done the video yet, before going into a rant about how much of a stuck-up prick I was and that he'd never watch anything I did again. Now, I don't care about that, and I think it's probably a positive to not have that man as a fan, but the only reason he got so furious is because social media gave him the sense he was entitled to contact me and that I should be compelled to respond and meet his demands.

There are reasons why these platforms are addictive, though, and I have to confess to having found them extremely useful during lockdown. Social media enabled people to feel connected in a way that they could not otherwise. It enabled people to share information and it was even through social media that we were able to pretend that we cared about NHS workers by clapping at our front doors for 30 seconds once a week until that became boring.

It feels obvious to state that we are on our phones too much. I haven't seen a horror film anywhere near as frightening as my iPhone's screen-time reports. I have genuinely reached the stage where I've had to start factoring extra hours into my work day because I know I'll get distracted by the phone and be unable to resist my compulsion to check social media. I downloaded an app called Forest where you plant a virtual tree that grows for the duration that you leave your phone untouched. If you go on to your phone, the tree dies. I know it sounds fairly ridiculous that it has taken an imaginary tree to keep my willpower in check, but what can I tell you? I'm devastated when one of those little fuckers dies.

I have tried to get myself into the mindset of seeing my phone as a treat rather than a default distraction, although it's been a fucking nightmare staying off it while writing this book. In a bid to break my habit I've even tried leaving it at home when I go out, although this means that you spend the entire day convinced that everyone you know has died in a fire and nobody has been able to tell you. I am also dabbling with the idea of having weekends off, but Leesa and the kids would only be sitting on their phones anyway so there seems little point. If any of this rings true to you and you want to let me know how you are getting on with your phone addiction, feel free to tweet me and tell me – I will almost definitely be on there, but I might not reply.

Football

I love Arsenal football club. I have since I was ten years old, and I have spent untold amounts of money on shirts, tickets, and beers watching them. I realize this is what everyone does and actually, as fans go, I would definitely describe myself on the milder end of the scale, despite nearly crying on the day Thierry Henry left the club. I suspect that says more about my mental state than anything else but let's keep it light.

The truth is, though, and I might get slaughtered for saying this, but keeping up with the club has recently felt more of a chore. Ten years ago, I would get myself to as many games as possible. I used to love the build-up to a match. From Crawley to north London, you're looking at the best part of a three-hour round trip, but that meant 180 minutes of chatting, drinking and soaking up the atmosphere with other fans and whoever I was with. It felt like a pilgrimage. Now it feels like a ball-ache. When I do make it to games, the whole day out serves to entrench my belief that there are very few experiences that beat not doing them and staying at home instead.

It doesn't help that if you support a Premier League club there will always be a way of watching the game on television or the internet. This makes justifying the journey increasingly difficult. People will say you're missing the atmosphere. I'm not sure if the crowd of 60,000 is that much better than hearing an amateur commentator shout 'Goal!' at the top of his lungs on an illegal stream. It is for that reason, therefore, that I started falling out of love with going to watch the football. It became too easy to stay at home.

The other issue I have is that I have become too busy and my brain has become too confused to retain all the various bits of information – stats, match permutations, potential transfers, formation issues, injury lists – that properly supporting a football club requires. It only serves to feed my dementia paranoia when I'm discussing Arsenal with a mate and they point out to me that I hadn't figured out that if we get a draw on Tuesday and Chelsea get two yellow cards then we still have a 30 per cent chance of qualifying for the Champions League. I just do not have the spare brainpower to stay across that when I'm trying to figure out how to stop my children saying 'vagina' loudly in public.

I wondered if it meant that I didn't like football any more, but whenever I do watch a game, I love it as much as I always have. I have just become too lazy to process all of the moving parts. For the same reason, I resent Marvel for forcing me to remember so many bits and pieces from previous films in order to understand what's going on. My headspace has finite capacity and if I have to remember all the negotiations of Arsenal's four transfer targets, I might forget I'm supposed to pick up the kids from school.

This has also become apparent with new interests I

assumed I would have more enthusiasm for. For example, I got into basketball this year. That sport is unbelievable. It has everything: exciting dunks, excellent footwear, great music, and every single game almost without exception is thrilling. I discovered my love for the sport when filming the second series of *Rob and Romesh Versus*. As soon as I returned from filming, I downloaded the NBA app and began to watch as many games as I possibly could. However, it started to become clear that, particularly as I wasn't following a specific team, there were way too many fixtures to stay on top of. I genuinely started to become stressed when I logged on to the app and saw the number of games I had to catch up on. We would get to the end of the day and I'd tell Leesa I needed some time apart so I could get caught up on what I'd missed. I even began to get nervous when people asked me about my new sport because I knew I had fallen behind and might not be able to field their questions.

It's even become slightly true of hip-hop. I am hip-hop obsessed, and it forms a small part of my job through my *Hip-Hop Saved My Life* podcast. Nevertheless, I find it a huge effort to stay across all the new music that's released. Sometimes, somebody will mention an album that is apparently excellent. Rather than being excited about listening to a great new record, I put the name of the album on a list of things I have to do, and something I love becomes a task to get done. It sucks a little bit of the joy out of it. I imagine most people experience this to some extent, where you get so busy that staying up to speed with a passion becomes more of a hassle than a pleasure.

I really don't want football to be like that, but, honestly, I'm starting to feel like following Arsenal is more of an investment situation: you need to put in a lot in order to enjoy the returns. When Arsenal did the double in 2001 I went to so many games, watched any I couldn't get to on TV, and followed that team like it was my job. I put Arsenal stuff all over my car and me and my friends drove around like very polite hooligans. When we went on to win the title and the FA Cup, I genuinely felt I had had a role to play in those victories. A very small part of them was mine. I don't think those successes would have felt as sweet if I had been a casual fan during that season, so I fully appreciate the rewards you get from throwing all your energy behind a football team, and I want my children to experience that too.

A few years ago, I took my son to watch Arsenal versus Chelsea in the FA Cup final. I remember feeling a little bit dirty as I hadn't really been to any games that season and so I didn't feel like I had earned the right to attend the final. Fortunately, I was able to use the excuse of giving my son an experience he wouldn't forget to assuage my guilt.

My intermittent support aside, game days are now a slightly different experience for me because people often recognize me. I really don't mind people coming up and asking for photos or wanting to shake hands (deadly viruses permitting). In fact, sometimes when my kids comment on how much it happens, I remind them that the real worry will be when it stops. Going to an FA Cup final is what I would describe, in terms of people asking for photos, as an absolute fuck-fest. People are drunk, charged up for the game, and have no qualms about asking for a photo or, even, appraising your entire career in front of you. It tempers your enjoyment of the day somewhat, when a bloke decides to tell you exactly where you rank in their list of comedians.

It was an amazing game, with Arsenal winning against the odds, which is the best type of victory. You could argue that it's almost worth your team being a bit crap because when they do get a win it is that much sweeter. I will always remember a bloke tapping me on the shoulder at the end of the game, gesturing to my son and saying, 'What an amazing experience for him. I didn't bring my son because I wanted to really enjoy the day if we won,' meaning that he wanted to get absolutely battered. Strange bloke. And the day felt strange too. Winning the FA Cup didn't feel like something I could claim as mine in the way I could other victories in the past. You have to do the hard yards to feel the benefits. You feel like it's you that's been to training when you have stood in the freezing rain and watched your team get annihilated.

So now I find myself in the position of trying to decide what type of football fan I will be going forward. Am I going to be the guy who forgoes family events to head out every week to shout for the team through thick and thin, going on the glorious campaign, cheering the players through the rollercoaster that is a season, knowing that it might all be for nothing? Or am I going to become the annoying part-timer who watches it all on TV and then tries to get tickets for the big games like a proper prawn-sandwich prick?

This dilemma feels all the more important because of how I came to follow football in the first place. When I was growing up, my dad didn't take me to any games, I think because as an immigrant Asian man he didn't feel comfortable going. In British culture men are almost expected to love football. And I have heard so much racism at games, and I remember my dad telling me horrendous stories about stuff he encountered, as well as seeing it for myself, so for a while I found it tricky to get behind the sport. It was difficult to support a team alongside a bunch of people who hated you. My dad told me he once walked into a pub when a game was on, found he was the only Asian man there, and they all started singing 'Vindaloo' at him. To be fair, racism aside, that's pretty funny, but the truth is it's rank, and is something I'm glad I don't encounter as often now, despite the fact that football still harbours numerous bell-ends and is still addressing its racist associations.

So my dad didn't bring me up watching football, but I found it myself, and then he took an interest in my passion. We went to the football together, and I value those times so highly that I want to create them with my kids. However, as the boys get older, they see I'm not as passionate about it as I once was, and their interest wanes as a result. Increasingly, they would rather watch YouTube than Arsenal. I try to counteract this by showing them YouTube videos of great Arsenal goals, but I feel like I'm forcing them to engage with it.

This to me has highlighted the fact that us supporting Arsenal is actually pretty useful – it's a thing we can all get into and engage with. It's quality time. We need to see football as less me going and occasionally taking one of them with me and more as a family activity that brings us all together. And it's about this time that I reveal this entire chapter has mainly been about me convincing Leesa to let me get season tickets for the whole family.

Race Relations

It is incredibly difficult to comment on racism without being accused of not fully appreciating the nuances, or, worse still, being racist yourself. I sometimes find myself feeling sorry for well-meaning white people who are genuinely ignorant of the existence of discrimination and then, when they ask a question that betrays that ignorance, are ridiculed. Don't get me wrong, I think it's important for people to be better informed on the subject, but the public shaming that takes place when someone trips up over the correct terminology or displays a poor grasp of the issue makes it even more difficult for people to talk about it.

The exception here is when people use that ignorance as a defence for some fairly unsavoury opinions, or as a means of denying that a problem exists. On *The Ranganation*, I explained that I thought it was ignorant to counter the slogan of Black Lives Matter with the slogan All Lives Matter. People claim they are saying it from a position of equality, but what they are actually doing is being resentful of the accusations of inequality and racism that they feel are being levelled at them. It's a deflection, and it prevents people from facing the real issue head on.

Weirdly, I find it pretty comparable to the behaviour of

non-vegans. When Gregg's brought out the vegan sausage roll, there were no meat ranges under threat, there was absolutely zero potential issue for regular customers of Gregg's, but still there was outrage. People were angry it was being called a sausage roll, people were annoyed that Gregg's had decided to cater for the vegan, and social media was ablaze with how ridiculous this all was.

I really do feel this is a symptom of guilt. People know that veganism is an ethical option, but vegan food being shit and difficult to get hold of means that you have a ready excuse for not changing your diet. Then they start making viable vegan options readily available and you start finding yourself facing the fact that the reason you're eating meat is that it's delicious and you don't want to give it up. I totally get that. But people seem to feel threatened by the presence of an alternative, as if their choices are under question. As a result, they go on the defensive.

Similarly, when people highlight the issue of discrimination and the inequalities of society, we are all forced to confront something that it is much easier to ignore. If people find this too uncomfortable, they have the choice of either admitting they know there's inequality but do nothing about it, or finding reasons why the inequality is being invented or exaggerated, and why they are in fact the one being discriminated against, which gives them a sense of righteousness and assuages any potential guilt. These people are called pricks. But their self-centred response is human nature, and that defensiveness is understandable. Tempting as it is to highlight their bias and shout some sense into them, there is an argument that

239

trying to call these people out for being stupid and ignorant might not be the way to improve the situation. Or at least not totally.

I didn't say anything like this on *The Ranganation* because that show does not exist for me to inflame political debate. I just made a series of jokes about how ridiculous a notion it was to keep shouting All Lives Matter rather than examining the reasons why people feel so passionately about shouting Black Lives Matter. I simply pointed out that it might be better to engage with why people are angry rather than googling to see if black people were ever slave owners so you can find a loophole through which to dismiss the entire BLM movement.

When the show went out, I received a lot of messages from people saying they were happy I had said all that, but a number of people also got in touch to say they were furious. Bizarrely, one of the messages went something like, 'Enjoy what you do, and I like the show, but All Lives do Matter.' Now, obviously I disagree with that sentiment, but I did find the message slightly heartening. At a time when people are so volatile when their opinions are challenged, the fact somebody was able to watch me say that, strongly disagree and yet still enjoy the show, and then send me a cordial message afterwards, actually meant a lot. We really do need to get better at respectfully disagreeing with each other.

There was one man in particular who didn't get that memo. He got in touch with me on Facebook to tell me that all lives do matter, and he went on to say that if he heard me saying anything like that again, 'Honestly I will kill you.' I cannot even begin to imagine what series of events and experiences have combined to make somebody so violently angry about the slogan Black Lives Matter, let alone about my personal take on it. Imagine watching somebody suggest that it was a good thing to listen to the Black Lives Matter movement, and being so angered by that sentiment that you message that person to threaten their life.

That threat level is something I worry about. My children hear racist comments from kids at their school and I know that means those children have heard those views from their friends or their parents. That, combined with the fact these kids are just kids, makes it difficult to bring attention to the problem. People don't want to believe their kids are doing anything wrong, least of all if it reflects badly on them as a parent or as a human being. One of our friends' children said something hideously racist to our son and he came back and told us fairly matter-of-factly what had been said. When my wife spoke to the mum about it, she was so defensive that she got shirty with Leesa for bringing it up in the first place.

This sort of playground racism really bothers me. You can see discriminatory views being passed down like an inheritance. It makes it impossible to feel optimistic about ending racism because I cannot begin to understand how you tackle it. Do you have to assign everyone one standard-issue friend of colour so they can eventually see that we can all get along?

One solution has been to encourage people to be anti-racist, actively rooting out racism and challenging it at source, as opposed to simply being passively non-racist in your views. This is surely a good idea, but I don't think it's particularly helpful to shout 'racist' at everyone you encounter. That's not the way to make progress, despite the fact that it does feel great. People now have such entrenched views that labels and accusations only fuel their levels of indignation. They become even more committed to their standpoint.

All this begs two questions: why am I even discussing this in what is supposed to be a light-hearted book about adult life, and what's my big solution?

In truth, a book about life has to tackle this issue. As I write this, the world is faced with an urgent need to address the deep divisions and the inherent racism in our society. Black Lives Matter has become the largest civil-rights movement in history, with millions peacefully protesting and speaking out about the issue all over the world. A minority of these protests have turned violent and have exposed the ugliness at the heart of the issue, with white nationalist groups, thugs and abusive law-enforcement officers facing off against BLM campaigners. To the moderate observer, you could be forgiven for thinking we are on the verge of some sort of race war. I had always hoped my children would grow up in a time when divisions between ethnic minorities were getting more and more eroded, but at the moment they have never been more obvious. The reality is that kids have said racist things to them on multiple occasions and just this week I have had to spend time explaining the protests to them.

It is for these reasons that I think it's hugely important

for all of us to think about exactly what we are telling our children. I have plenty of my own baggage when it comes to racism, and I don't want to pass that on, but there is a clear need to equip our children with a certain amount of knowledge and to prepare them for whatever they might encounter themselves. I sometimes feel hopeful that the cries of 'Go back to where you come from' and 'Take Britain back' are on the decline, but I have seen more of this in the last year than ever before, so it's inevitable my children will encounter these views. Admittedly I am a brown man on television and that is annoying for racists, so in that way I am a bit of a cunt beacon, but I really do think there are significant numbers of angry and intolerant people in the world and we need to have a strategy to deal with them.

I think there is blame on both sides. I confess to finding the demand that everybody respond to the issues immediately or be labelled 'complicit' ridiculous and unhelpful. Being forced to put together a standpoint or retweet something because you feel you have to is not constructive. Social media is not a place conducive to considered reflection.

I have also spoken to white people who don't feel they are racist but are terrified of being accused of it. I do feel for those people, but that is perception only. Most people are not of the belief that all white people are racist, and I would say a little short-term discomfort for people about looking racist is a small price to pay for what is hopefully an attitudinal sea change in how we view race relations and integration.

One of the most depressing things I have found about

the Black Lives Matter protests and subsequent fallout is that people I thought were tolerant and equality-minded have shown themselves to be on the side of the 'patriots'. These are not extreme right-wingers, but people I have spent a lot of time with who casually say things about how thuggish the BLM protesters have been and how our colonial statues needed protecting by what were just peaceful men trying to preserve our country's history.

I have a lot of issues with this. First, there were pricks on both sides, and we shouldn't judge each side by their most violent participants. I completely agree with that. In my opinion, the majority of BLM protesters turned up to support equality, whereas the response protest were a bunch of people doing Nazi salutes and, in the absence of the enemy they turned up to battle with, they turned on the police. But that's me showing the bias that I'm complaining about. The difference is, however, that I am correct.

In my opinion, we have to make society more equal, we have to force changes in thinking where people have become lazy, and we have to ensure that future generations are going to see an anti-racist standpoint be the absolute norm. And if there are people who have a problem with that, fuck 'em.

24 Hours to Live

One of the philosophical questions that keeps popping into my head is this: 'If you had 24 hours to live, what would you do?' (It's also a pretty average song by Mase.) I find the question fascinating. It uncovers what you consider to be your priorities, and also reveals that not everybody is going to be completely happy with your answer.

There is a lot to unpack with this question. For example, how are you going to die? Is it going to be instant? Is it going to be painful? Because if it's going to be painful, then I'm probably going to spend 23 hours and 58 minutes just kind of shitting myself about that.

The question also assumes you have your affairs in order. I have conversations with people of my age and I'm amazed at how prepared they are for death. They have all sorts of policies and investments in place so their families will be well looked after if they die. I am hugely disorganized. When I die, Leesa is basically going to have to get my wallet off my corpse and figure out the situation for herself. I'm also loath to set up too much to help her, as there's the obvious worry that you being dead becomes a more appealing prospect to those around you than you being alive. I am such a mess-generating slob that I think if

Leesa had less to clean up and a few lump sums headed her way, she might even start looking forward to my inevitable heart attack. I don't want my legacy to be her thinking she's won the fucking lottery.

So I reckon I would spend most of my final day trying to sort out a load of last-minute bits and pieces so Leesa and the kids were in the best possible position following my death, and also texting my mum to explain what I have set out in case in her enraged grief she assumes Leesa killed me for the pay-out. It's the sort of conclusion my mum could conceivably jump to.

There is a lot to glean just from your attitude to the news. There are people who have a never-say-die attitude and would spend their day trying to prevent that outcome from happening – people who would fight for their lives and really push to make sure they extend their time on this planet. I really don't have a lot of that in me. If somebody told me I had 24 hours to live, I'd be very accepting. I don't imagine people deliver that kind of news lightly, and 24 hours of doing stuff you want to do sounds a lot better than 23 and a half hours of trying to stay alive, and then half an hour of maybe getting a blow job to see you out, but then realizing that you may die during it and that isn't something you can leave somebody with the memory of, even if it does stop them doing it to anyone else after you're gone.

I have regularly told Leesa to get back on the horse immediately after I'm gone. My mum has not really seen anyone since my dad passed away, and I think she has been unhappier as a result. I'm sure my dad wouldn't mind – in fact, based on his behaviour when he was alive he would

have no bloody right to – but Mum retains a sense of loy-
alty to him in the back of her mind. I constantly tell Leesa
not to worry about this. Perhaps I do it too much. I'm half
expecting her to turn up at my funeral with her new man,
or worse still, not bother coming. But at that point, it will
be none of my concern.

Then there's the question of what you would actually
do, assuming all the admin was squared away – what's the
best way to spend your last hours? I suppose I'd want to
spend as much time as possible with the kids. But I'd also
want the day to be fun for them. I don't want their enduring memory of me to be that awful day we spent together
having a series of discussions about life. So we'd have to
pick something they wanted to do, which currently would
either be playing Fortnite or heading to a theme park.

I imagine going to a theme park might feel odd, knowing you're going to die later that evening. I imagine it
induces the type of acceptance of your fate that means
roller-coasters aren't really scary any more. Also, I find it
rage-inducingly annoying when I have to spend time queuing as it is, let alone when each hour-long queue represents
1/24th of the time I have left on the planet. There's a good
chance I'd end up being arrested for battering the shit out
of a queue-jumper.

Queue-jumping in its traditional sense doesn't happen
that much, but can I take this opportunity to say that if
you are one of those people who sends part of your group
to queue up and then joins them later on, you are unacceptable. I know you think it's fine because somebody
from your group has been waiting for you, but everyone

has made an assessment of the queue, and is counting down the minutes to getting to the front, and then you rock up at the last second to delay us just that little bit more, and everyone behind you who has had to let you squeeze past because you took time to grab an ice cream absolutely hates you and hopes you have the worst day ever. Unless of course you have some sort of disability, in which case people will analyse and discuss the disability and decide whether it's severe enough to not get angry about you going in front.

So, then we have to play videogames, which basically means an afternoon of me being repeatedly killed while the children shout at me for being a noob loser. I currently play games with them with the glimmer of hope I might get better, but this prospect being undermined by my imminent passing will make having my arse handed to me by the kids that much more irritating.

Then there's what to do with Leesa. For one thing, sex would be absolutely out of the window. I know a lot of people joke about spending the day having sex, but we'd have the kids with us, and I think even in my dying hours I would find it awkward to ask them for some private time so I can give their mum a seeing-to. Similarly, I want Leesa to have great memories of me. As time goes on, memories fade and you colour in the good times and fade out the bad. I don't think it's a good idea for one of her freshest memories to be me wheezing to a limping orgasm while wondering why I haven't taken off my Wu Tang socks.

My mum and brother would expect a visit so we'd have to have a family get-together, where I'd probably make them all eat vegan, just to annoy them with it one last time. They'd also then annoy me by dragging out their section of the day and leaving us with about twenty minutes.

One of the things I've discovered about myself is that although I pretend I don't want any fuss, I'm always slightly annoyed when there isn't one. On my last birthday I made Leesa promise she would do nothing for the day as I really don't give a shit about birthdays. She reluctantly agreed. Then, when the day rolled round, I spent the entire time wondering how she was going to go against my instructions. It turned out she wasn't. Even though I had specifically asked her to do exactly nothing, I got a bit shitty with her, but without being able to explain why because I knew I was being unreasonable, which is another reason why it's so great to live with me.

I imagine, therefore, that a lot of my last 24 hours would be spent wondering what surprise the family had lined up for me. I'd be expecting them to go all out on the last day of my life – I'm thinking The Roots come and do a private gig while I eat a 12-course meal of Sri Lankan and Thai cuisine, pausing only to visit the toilet and/or get a blow-job, during which The Roots would wait so I didn't miss any of my favourites. Then my old Maths teacher, who was a complete prick to me, would come and read out an apology. The evening would finish with me being paraded around on a chair like C–3PO at the end of *Return of the Jedi*, while The Roots do a series of 1990s hip-hop covers. I would also like to be wearing sunglasses as we party because I think it would be quite funny if every couple of songs they had to check if I was dead yet.

Endgame

What is the point of life? I am absolutely not the right person to answer that question, but it is something I have recently thought about a lot. I don't mean the big 'what is the point of existence' question, I mean more: what is the point of us doing anything? Why do we have jobs? Why do we have children? Why is it so important for us to buy a house? Are there people who have achieved everything they ever wanted to achieve and are now just chilling?

I write a column for the *Guardian* called 'Midlife Crisis'. The reason it's called this is mainly because they suggested it and I couldn't think of a better name. I've always felt it was a bit of a misnomer, however. Midlife crisis, to me, means that point where you wonder what the hell you've done with your life and then start heading on a completely different course. You decide to quit your job or leave your relationship, or maybe you just fantasize about doing these things and continue with your current set-up except more unhappily. I haven't ever worried about what I was doing with my life before, but the naming of that column got me thinking about it.

I don't know what my endgame is. I had a big change of career when I decided to stop being a teacher and become a comedian. But I had no plan beyond that. I didn't know what my comedy career goals were, and I didn't know why I was becoming a comedian beyond the fact that I enjoyed it a lot. I didn't have something that I was aiming for that meant I would know when I had achieved it. To be honest, my only real goal was to be able to pay the bills through doing comedy. And while I was incredibly grateful when that started to happen, that target is very much a moving one. Bills continue to come in, and comedy continues to be quite a fragile industry to be involved in. That is something I've said in interviews, and the interviewer has always said something like, 'I think you're going to be OK, haha.' And then all of a sudden a global pandemic happens and live performances are stopped almost immediately, so perhaps I was correct to be a little bit fucking worried? There is also quite a high probability that I will say something hugely inappropriate and just get cancelled. So I guess I have set myself a goal that can never really be achieved, which is probably the perfect recipe for dissatisfaction.

I've never thought of myself as somebody motivated by money. I realize this may come as a shock to people who think I say yes to every single TV show I'm offered, but to them I would say that, first, I do say no to things, and also I've never said yes to anything purely for the pay cheque. I've always tried to be driven by doing things that are enjoyable. I watched my father chase money his entire life, and he had periods when he succeeded and periods when he failed. I never really saw him happier, however, than when socializing with his mates, or spending time with his family, or going out for dinner with my mum. I genuinely believe that his ongoing quest to get a big house or to have a nice car, or any of those very basic signifiers of success, were things he did because he felt he was supposed to. He saw those things as ways of communicating to other people that he had achieved something. In the latter part of his life, he also felt pressure to make up for his previous mistakes. I really think, however, that if he just had enough money to go out when he wanted, buy cigarettes and pay for the taxi home, he would have genuinely been happy.

It is for these reasons, watching my dad's desire to make more money send him to prison, that I have tried to never make money my primary goal. Whenever you see these millionaires and billionaires living their lavish lifestyles, they are always still trying to make more money. Look at Jeff Bezos, a man for whom the global pandemic has been nothing but good news. You do have to wonder at this point, does this man have some compromising photos of God? There is no set of circumstances that lead to him failing. Having said that, I do find the fact that he is continuing to try to make money depressing. He has got more money than he could possibly spend over a thousand lifetimes. So why not chill out? Maybe that is what makes him happy. Maybe the ongoing quest for more and more money, despite the fact your wealth is growing at about the same rate as the opinion that you are a cunt, is the thing that gives you purpose.

You do find yourself asking why you are working. The ongoing conflict is that you make money so you can improve or maintain your quality of life. However, spending time working and being away from your family is one of the greatest possible downward drivers of your quality of life. Whenever I'm about to go away for work, I always feel horribly guilty. And then I will talk to someone who says something like, 'You're doing this for your family, don't feel bad.' And I wonder about that. Because to me it seems arse-about-face. I'm working now so I can provide for my family and by the time I've made enough money to retire, my kids will be grown up and won't give a shit about seeing me any more. That's without even factoring in them watching what I have said about them on stage and cutting me off anyway.

I've since become convinced that the way to achieve contentment is to first find a job you love, and then find a way to not be working so much that you don't enjoy your life as it goes by. I guess the point I'm trying to make is that I don't think enough of us stop to smell the roses. I've become aware that if you spend too much time trying to provide, trying to set your family up, trying to get yourself in a secure position, you end up missing out on the important stuff, neglecting the reasons you're doing all this in the first place.

When I first started doing comedy, we were completely and utterly broke. I remember going away with the family, having used vouchers to get there, and I would fill up as much as I possibly could on the included breakfast because we didn't have enough money for lunch. Now we are in a position where we can go on nicer holidays than that. But I wouldn't necessarily say we are having more fun now than we did back then. The children are a good indicator of this. I was able to save up enough money to take them on our amazing trip to Disneyland Paris. It was on the Eurostar home that I found the children discussing whether they preferred our week at the Disneyland Hotel or our trips to Butlin's in Bognor Regis. Obviously I am not trying to slight Butlin's, it is a great institution and they've nailed family fun. But in my head I saw the trip to Disneyland as this breakthrough moment where I had enough money to provide an incredible experience for my family, whereas they just saw it as a holiday like any other.

I had a weird experience at Butlin's. When you work in comedy, you can get recommended for jobs from strange sources. On one occasion, I received an email from a movie company. They were working on a brand-new action comedy film and had a first draft of the script ready. For some reason, somebody involved in the film had heard of me, and thought I might be the right person to funny up the script. I read the email, knowing there are probably many people more qualified than me to do that job. Nevertheless, I was intrigued. I went through the script and added notes where I thought they could have improved things.

I sent off the email and thought nothing more of it. Two days later, I received a reply from the studio explaining that they loved what I had done. They wanted to know if I could have a phone meeting with them and the execs involved in the movie so that they could hear my ideas first-hand. The only time they could have this meeting was when I was due to be at Butlin's for the weekend with my family. Obviously I wasn't going to cancel my trip to Butlin's. I was, however, fascinated to have this meeting.

I started to wonder if this was going to be the sort of mad story that ended with me writing the new Star Wars.

I think we had just finished watching the Fireman Sam show when it was time for me to make my call. I walked over to the reception at Butlin's and joined the Hollywood meeting via my phone. The guy from the film studio did indeed have all the execs with him in the room. He started explaining how they were super keen to hear what else I could bring to the film. I was almost certain this was some sort of prank. On the other hand, I was possibly about to become a movie mogul from the comfort of my Butlin's holiday, and I had no intention of bailing out.

Where it started to go wrong was when it became clear my contact at the studio had overstated my level of experience to the execs. They seemed to be under the impression I was able to fix any and all issues with the storyline. For example, they asked me whether I had any ideas about what to use as a McGuffin instead of the nuclear codes they had in the script. I had absolutely no fucking idea what they should've done instead. I should've explained that. I should've explained that I work in comedy and that's the limit of my expertise. But, and it might have been the heady atmosphere at Butlin's, I instead attempted to freestyle a solution. I started describing a possible idea where they could use some sort of computer virus as the McGuffin and that the bad guy in the film could be planning to unleash it on to the world. As I write that now, it does seem ridiculous, but I figured that since they once released a successful film where the two main characters swapped faces, this seemed fairly normal by comparison. I

was starting to think about who my Hollywood neighbours would be when they inevitably asked me to move.

Unfortunately for me, I must have not explained it
that convincingly. My contact at the studio immediately
sounded a lot less confident, and possibly embarrassed. He
told me they would consider my idea and they were very
grateful for my time and would be in touch as soon as possible. What I suspect happened was that, as I was delivering
my pitch from Bognor Regis, the execs around the table in
LA started looking at each other as if they were getting
movie advice from an idiot. Which was fairly close to
the truth.

Film is something I'd love to do one day. In my darker
moments I wonder if one day in the future I'll be embark-
ing on filming my first starring role in a Hollywood comedy
when a man I've never seen before but whose voice sounds
familiar says something like, 'This is that wanker who tried
to pretend to be a movie expert on the phone.' And then
my dream will be dead. All because I got carried away on
holiday.

So, Romesh, I hear you ask, are you suggesting that the
meaning of life is spending your money wisely when you
go away?

It certainly looks like that, doesn't it? Obviously that is
not a point I'm trying to make. I guess what I'm trying to
say is that your happiness doesn't increase proportionately
to the amount of money thrown at it. And if that's the
case, then is the chase for money that has become our idea
of success really worth it?

When I was broke, I wasn't fantasizing about being in a

position where I could buy loads of nice shit. What I was fantasizing about was not panicking every time the bills came in at the end of the month. I remember getting to a point where every time I thought about money I would feel some sort of anxiety. Earning enough money to regularly cover the bills is probably the most elated I have ever felt financially. After that, all of my favourite moments have been centred around spending time with my family in whatever circumstance that may be.

This leads to the big question of what you tell your children. Everything about our lives is geared up to teaching kids that they have to gain qualifications so that they can get a decent enough job that will allow them to be financially comfortable. Our children spend six hours of every weekday and time in the evenings completely devoted to that eventual target. There's an argument that a lot of this education is being delivered for the intrinsic value of learning about things in the first place. But it all then moves towards a series of tests that assess how much you've retained and your life choices are affected accordingly.

Every time I fully engage with the idea of what exactly it is that we should be delivering to children in order to best prepare them for life, I can't help thinking we're getting it wrong. It is for that reason that I find it very tricky to push my children when they are not enjoying something academically. We ask them to apply themselves fully and support them as much as possible but without ever making them feel like the results of what they do at school are incredibly important. Admittedly, we will truly have no idea whether this is a good idea or not until it is too late, and all three of them will either do well or be utterly shagged by our strategy. It would probably have been a better idea to treat one of them as a control variable. What I'm ultimately hoping, though, is that they find what it is that makes them happy as soon as they possibly can and then follow that path. If that path is supporting Chelsea football club, I'll be really fucked off.

Acknowledgements

There are a few people without whom this book would not have been possible, and I would love to thank them now, both because I probably won't do it in person, and also because my publisher told me it looks bad if you don't.

To Leesa: thank you for being so supportive of everything I do, or at least as supportive as you can be without watching or reading any of it. You are one of the best humans I know, and when you leave, I won't even resent you. It's like when Thierry Henry left Arsenal, you just want the best for the person you love. I guess what I am saying is, I am grateful to be your stopgap until you find your FC Barcelona.

To the boys, Theo, Alex and Charlie: you are the most incredible set of human beings I have ever met, but I am hardwired biologically to think that. You are far better children than I have any right to have in my life, and I am thoroughly grateful for every single minute I get to spend in your company, even when you are banging on about Fortnite. I love you with all my heart. Can you please flush the toilet after you have a shit?

To Mum: thanks for being the wonderful supportive person you are, and for always being up for being in all of the stuff I ask you to do with me, even though we both know you are just pretending to be supportive and are actually doing it so you can become a celebrity. I will never be able to repay you for what you have done for us. Emotionally, I mean. Financially, I'm pretty sure you owe *me* money. Love you, Mum.

Dinesh: you are the person I look up to most in the world. You're smart, loyal, charming, good-looking, and an absolute twat when you're drunk. I'll be honest, I wrote a really good one of these for you in the last book, so do you want to just go and have a look at that? Thanks for remaining slim and attractive just to hammer home how I haven't – prick. Love you, bro.

To Flo: thanks for being such a great agent as well as one of my best friends. Your ongoing support, as well as your ability to cope with the fact that I'm unable to retain even the most basic information is something I could not do without – I really would not be working in comedy without you. Thank you for everything you do, cuzi.

To Dad: I'm not sure how this works really, as you're dead and so unless there is a Waterstones in heaven or wherever you are then this seems slightly pointless, and it does beg the question as to who exactly I'm writing this for. We miss you every single day, and even though as time goes on I struggle to remember exactly what your voice sounded like, I will never forget how terrible you were at dancing. Dreadful. I love you, Dad. Hope you're proud. Of us. Not the dancing – that really was fucking awful.

ABOUT THE AUTHOR

Romesh Ranganathan is a stand-up comedian and actor. A former maths teacher, he made his comedy circuit debut in 2010, and has quickly established himself as one of British comedy's brightest stars.

Romesh appears frequently on multiple TV and radio shows, is the star of *Asian Provocateur*, *The Misadventures of Romesh Ranganathan* and *The Ranganation*, and is a regular panellist on *A League of Their Own*. He writes occasionally for the *Guardian*.